Stories of a boy
dreams a...

OH, WHAT A TRIP!

JEFFREY A. ROHR

20 Twenty
Literary Group

Oh, What a Trip!
Copyright © 2023 by Jeffrey A. Rohr

All rights reserved. No part of this publication may be reproduced, distributed, or transmitted in any form or by any means, including photocopying, recording, or other electronic or mechanical methods, without the prior written permission of the author, except in the case of brief quotations embodied in critical reviews and certain other non-commercial uses permitted by copyright law.

ISBN
978-1-961250-69-7 (Paperback)
978-1-961250-70-3 (eBook)
978-1-961250-68-0 (Hardcover)

OH, WHAT A TRIP!

TABLE OF CONTENTS

The Swamp Rats 1

Childs Play or Life Lessons 8

The Canoe 12

Freedom-Dumb or Not? 16

Five Men in a Tub 20

Spring Break 22

College Buddies, Bats, and Flood 29

The First Canadian Trips (The learning Process) 33

Second Canadian Trip (Trash Mobile) 36

Three Band Members and a Friend 45

Biting Off More than You Can Chew 50

Mellen 54

Lots of Naked Girls on a Rock 59

Quest 63

Bang! 67

GMC	73
How to wreck a friend's canoe	81
The Times they are a Changing	88
Bill M.	91
Tuck Well	93
Planetarium	97
Canada	99
Group Ream Out	109
Ben and Mark Brave the Wild	111
Back on the River	113
Lay Over Day	116
On Our Own	120
Moosonee	127
Cochrane	130
Hitting the Road	132
Reality Check	138
Pittsburg	141
New Canoe and Gear	145
Trip Planning	155
Meramec River Missouri	160
Now What?	167

Allenwater River 170

Wilderness Emergency or Stupidity? 174

Canoe? 179

Orienteering 187

Home 190

Reflections 191

THE SWAMP RATS

It started at an early age, the allure of the wild, when my older brother and his friends started the Swamp Rats. We lived in a suburb of Chicago in the Fifties and it is hard to believe now, because the city has swallowed it up. It once had lots of wild country for a bunch of normal but bit wild kids, *"no not a bit"*, I mean *"wild"* to root around in. I am little over a year younger than my brother and grew up sharing a room, which lead to many battles, but also friendship, and I conned my way into the club, basically, because my brother was the wildest and toughest of the bunch. I am Jeff Rohr and I have lived life as a canoe guide, instructor, and musician, and continue to live a life of many excellent adventures. I hope you get a chuckle, and a bit of wisdom, out of these stories which I am about to reveal to all. Remember, real life is much more incredible than any fiction.

I have to be careful here not to freak out my 90-year-old mother and other mothers when they read the tales I'm about to divulge. I will edit some of the more horrifying actions of the Swamp Rats, though you may not believe that after reading those included. I will not name names because I'm not sure the statute of limitations has expired and as a Swamp Rat, "don't you know", we do have a code.

Our swamp consisted of a large area compete with several ponds surrounded by swamp, cattails and forest. We hunted, trapped, and amused ourselves with lots of devilish things that made sense to us kids at the time. Having a club meant that we, of course, had to have a tree house, and of course it had to be high. Being kids, we had no idea how to build one, but we managed with only one rat falling out of his roost as he stepped on a forgotten to be nailed board. Luckily, we were in the swamp which cushioned his fall; a good laugh was had by all until all of us had to take the plunge, because of our macho Rat pride.

We loved winter in the swamp because it was mostly frozen making travel easier. We figured a true test of one's manhood was to brave the thin ice. We made a game out of crawling on our bellies on the thin ice, anticipating that heart pounding moment when the ice would break, plunging us into the shock of breath-taking cold water. Unfortunately, I was good at this game, being the youngest and smallest at the time, but being good at this game was not a great thing. I have many memories of great terror and harrowing trips home trying to beat the debilitating freezing of the clothes with the knowledge of how difficult walking would soon become. The other alternative was to make a fire and attempt to dry our clothes. This method had some real downsides; first taking your wet clothes off in the cold, and second, the extreme possibility of setting your clothes on fire. This was a hard thing to explain to a very miffed mother when she asked where our socks went and why the rest of your clothes were singed black. I get a chuckle to this day when I see some of my clients attempting this procedure, and the folly of their actions.

The swamp had a good population of muskrats, minks, snakes, rabbits, frogs, birds - well you get the idea, and they all fell prey to us in one way or the other. Muskrats and minks, we trapped, and if we caught one on the ice, well let us just say, some of the rats may have gone a little savage on them. We had an outlet for skins with the most valuable being mink. It made sense, to us devil kids, that when we saw a trap with a mink in it, which happened not to be our trap, that we took the liberty of making it our own. We learned a valuable lesson one day when an older trapper showed up at our house. He was not a happy camper with some punk kids stealing his mink out of his trap and screwing up the skinning. Our defense, to our very angry Dad, was that it was our swamp and he was invading it. That argument did not work well at all! Those were the good old days when kids learned to respect their elders, the hard way.

Rabbits also fell prey to us entrepreneurial kids. There was a restaurant in the neighborhood, that served hasenpfeffer (rabbit) and gave us two bucks for each of them. That was decent money back then and would feed two Rats at one of the first McDonalds, only a couple of miles away. The technique that we used consisted of two lines of Swamp Rats in a snow-covered field walking toward each other armed with clubs. The snow had to be at least a foot deep. We would spook the rabbits, and they would run a short distance and borrow in the snow and - you can figure out the rest. One time it got interesting, the rabbit ran into a low area where the snow had blown making a bowl with a Rat in close pursuit. The Rat had lost his club during the chase, - well there goes that savage thing again. This would have made a great video, except for exposing the identity of the psycho Rat. Are you mortified yet? You might think all of us would turn out to be serial killers and not upstanding citizens, which, for some of us may be a matter of opinion.

We really liked snakes, as Rats, and would catch any that we could get our hands on. One of the macho Rat things that we did, as Rats, is to let a garter snake chomp down on us. Not too smart, but it was very macho! It hurts like hell and they don't like to let go! There is a reason to be frightened of snakes. One day, my brother, a couple of Rats and I came upon, believe it or not, a fox snake is part of the rat snake family; A BIG FOX RAT SNAKE! It was at least six feet long, big, fat and impressively strong. It took five Rats to pull it out of the brush after an epic struggle that went down in RAT history. The thing about a fox snake is it looks just like a rattlesnake, except without the rattle, and knows it. It mimics a rattler by rattling its tail on a leaf or anything available. It just so happened that our grandmother, who grew up in Montana and was now living with us to watch over us, (Ha!) allowing both our parents to work to make enough money to try to feed us, which was difficult, was extremely afraid of snakes. Well, you probably know what is coming next, but here goes. We went home, got a box, put the snake in it and closed the lid. Now remember, I already said we were very wild and devilish kids, so do not freak out, it was all in fun, except maybe for our very sweet grandmother, who opened the box after our insistent prompting, turned white, couldn't breathe, and almost fainted. We were sure she was having a heart attack. We had no good defense with our very mad parents about this one, and once again had sore asses for a few days. Although, it turned out good for the snake, which we were forced to set free.

One of the things that, hopefully, we all learn as we get older is that bad things can happen by poor choices. Well, here is a doozy. In the summer in the swamp, the cattails would grow to epic heights making travel in the swamp very difficult. We were trying to alleviate this problem by cutting paths in the cattails, which proved to be very difficult. So, one of the enterprising Rats, again no names, came up with what we all thought was a brilliant idea; we could use fire to burn paths through the cattails. We knew, because it was late summer and the cattails were nice and dry, it wouldn't be hard to start a fire. We just had to control the burn to make some nice beautiful paths to enhance our Rat travel. The swamp butted up against the back of the subdivision, where most of us lived. Specifically, one of the Rat's houses was one of these. Again, you probably already have figured out what happened. It took only minutes after starting the fire for it to get completely out of control. Even we seasoned devilish Rats were impressed by the height of the flames. Not surprisingly, it was not long before us Rats, enjoying the fire and thinking of getting some hot dogs, were joined by three companies of Firemen who worked frantically to save all the houses and put out the fire. Now, being smart grownups of course looked at us with the utmost of suspicion and grilled us hard with no luck. They should have known that us Rats don't squeal! UH! OH! Hope no Rats read this and hope the statute of limitations has run out!

I do not know how we darling kids pulled off getting pump action daisy BB guns from our dads. Remember the thing about choices! Well, he was a good Dad and he trusted us kids. Do not know why, but he did. The rule was we could not go out of the yard with the BB guns. Little did he know how that rule was followed? NOT! Some of the RATS, including my brother, played gunslinger on any bird in their sights, except for songbirds, and kept track of their kills by burning iron dots on the plastic buts of their guns. Sorry Bro! You don't want to know what the winning number was. This is that devilish thing again. Well on with the story. A neighbor, whose house was just across the drainage ditch separating the yards, came over and accused us sweet kids of putting a BB hole in one of his back windows. My Dad, being a trusting father, which of course we taught him not to be, but later on that, stood up for us and claimed, because we were not allowed to go out of the yard, that no way could a BB gun put a hole in his window at that distance and was hell bent on proving it. *"Way to go DAD."* He told my brother, *"Go get that old piece of glass and your BB gun and we'll see who's right about this."* Remember that choices thing! He walked about fifty feet away, held the glass to his side and told my brother to shoot the glass. Keep in mind that it was my brother who won the bird-shooting contest. Oops! My brother claimed that he took careful aim, shot and watched the BB curve right into our dad's leg, who promptly screeched, bolted for the house, pulled his pants down and checked for damage. Oh, for a video camera! Meanwhile, my brother and I were trying hard to hide the laughter that was trying to burst out of us. The amazing thing is that he believed my brother, who claimed the BB, to his dismay, curved right into his leg. Maybe it did! Well, he paid the neighbor and took our BB guns away for a while. In case you're wondering, he wasn't hurt badly. We knew that because another one of the macho things that we did was to shoot each other! There's that choices thing again.

It was interesting that a customer, who became a good friend, showed up at our resort for some camping and canoeing and even went on to take canoe lessons and a longer canoe trip with us. We were sitting around the fire shooting the crap after cooking a great meal over the fire when the subject of where we grew up came up. I couldn't believe it; we both grew up in Lombard in the very same subdivision but he was five years younger. He then put two and two together and said, *"You were one of the Swamp Rats, weren't you? You guys scared the crap out of us kids."* I was mortified by his statement. My memories did not include terrorizing any younger kids but could understand how a bunch of older kids who hung around in a gang and would often be carrying guns, even though they were only BB guns, might make a big impression on a five-year-old. I apologized to him for any trauma that we may have caused and he just laughed and said, *"We were just kids then and we really only wanted to be just like you."* Then he said," *You're not going to shoot me are you."* I just laughed and hoped he was only joking.

We learned many things early on in our life exploring the swamp. First, it's not fun to fall through thin ice. Second, it is hard to walk with frozen clothes. Third, drying clothes over a fire is an iffy proposition, but sometimes necessary. Fourth, snakes are dangerous but can be fun to play with. Fifth, dads sometimes can be cool and it is dangerous to get them mad. Sixth, hanging in a gang will antagonize younger kids but will make them want to follow in your footsteps, "so all you kids out there, realize the power that you are wielding and be careful." Last, but not the least, if you want excellent memories, you have to have excellent adventures.

CHILDS PLAY OR LIFE LESSONS

It is amazing how the things we are exposed to as kids shape our lives. I hope you get a chuckle out of some of the stories that help mold my life. One Christmas I asked my parents for some skis, and low and behold, I got a pair. They were a cross between a downhill ski and a cross-country ski and did not come with any poles. The binding was a bungee strap that connected you to the ski, similar to a snowshoe binding.

We had a steep back yard that ended in a steep drop to a drainage ditch. I remember vividly the first time on the skis, which was a kamikaze terror run toward the ditch ending in a spectacular fall. What a blast! I was hooked. After awhile I got the hang of crashing, finally learned to stop, and soon got bored. Our house had a carport with a steep drop that terminated into a retaining wall after about eight feet. It was made of these two by four feet rectangular clay drainage tiles keeping the soil from sliding down into the back yard.

I remember the weekend that my uncle came up to help put up the wall. My uncle was a part time county sheriff, hunted and loved guns. He taught my brother and me how to shoot and exposed us to hunting. He owned so many guns that he stored them under all the furniture in his and our aunt's house. This used to bug the heck out of my aunt who was continually surprised by all manner of different guns she discovered while cleaning. He was a big man with a big gut and serious demure, a perfect image of a county sheriff.

My brother, Dad, Uncle, and I were working hard putting in these big clay tiles when suddenly, my big macho Uncle began this bizarre frantic jig and began to scream. *"Somethings in my Pants. Help! Help!"* He proceeded to rip off his overalls with great gusto and this little tiny mouse jumped out and the rest of us laughed our heads off. It was one of the funniest moments of my life; my big macho Uncle being brought down by this little mouse. It is a good thing that my uncle wasn't packing that day, because he would have probably shot himself going after that evil mouse and maybe us too.

I enjoyed watching the winter Olympics, especially the ski jumping, which I'm sure prompted the epiphany moment that the hill and the tiles would make a great ski jump.

There was a steep hill from our carport to the tiles then a straight drop down four feet and on down the hill. Up the hill, I went with visions of the Olympics in my future, got into the ski jump crouch, pushed off, and with surprising speed raced down the hill, off the cliff, and dropped like a stone in a spectacular crash. I thought I broke my skis and was sure my right ankle was broken. *"I guess it wasn't a perfect ski jump,"* I thought. I soon realized that my body and skis survived and went to find our snow shovel. I thought, *"If I pile up the snow so it wasn't such an abrupt drop maybe it would be better."* Again, a spectacular crash, but better. Then I piled up snow at the bottom before the drop to give me some more lift and tried it again. I got really good at crashing that day but finally, with more adjustments and many crashes, I made a jump and stayed upright. I had many fun days playing Olympic ski jumper and to this day, I still enjoy skiing, and even made a cross-country ski trail at our resort, spending many winter days zooming down the hills. Smartly, a long time ago, I gave up any thoughts of jumping down anything, especially with skis on.

One time I remember this rabbit, Uh Oh! Better, not tell this story. My Godfather Don lived next door and was an avid outdoorsman. He had only daughters and I was the son he never had so he would take me fishing. He also taught me how to spearfish with a bow. Let me qualify that. For me it was to "try" to spear a fish with a bow. This is an absurdly hard sport. Just think about trying to hit a moving fish with an arrow. You have to judge the depth of the fish, and compensate for the refraction of the arrow and the speed it is traveling. This is not easy to do. Don rigged my bow with a reel, taped it to the bow with a line attached to a special arrow with a barbed point. We spent many a day trying to hit fish with an arrow, which Don did, me, not so much, but it gave me a love for archery, and not surprisingly, I am now an avid bow hunter.

Dad and Don decided to take my brother and me on a fishing trip. We left for our trip with a little food, fishing gear and a couple of tents, and traveled up to a campground on a lake in Wisconsin. The cabin tent was for Don and Dad and the pup tent was for my brother and I. We left after Dad and Don got off work on a Friday and arrived at the campground just before dark. We set up the tents and went to bed. This was going to be the first time my brother and I had ever slept in a tent. It did not take long before we got scared, vacated the tent, and slept in the car. The next morning, we got a lot of good-natured ribbing from the laughing grownups who found us in the car. Later that day, I hooked into a giant 20lb carp making for an excellent day and great memories.

We camped again that night and Bruce and I successfully made it through the night. I still love to fish and camp.

My Dad was a little handy and I enjoyed helping him put up paneling and do simple projects around the house. He was a Honky Tonk piano player, started teaching me piano at eight, and quickly found me a piano teacher after I showed a real interest in playing. I remember the joy I felt playing the piano, and would spend endless hours improvising around a simple chord progression that I created and knew even then that music would always be a big part of my life. I started to play professionally at age 14, went to music school, taught piano and wrote music. I still feel the same joy today, that I felt when I was eight.

When my younger brother came along, and following my mother's itch to move every seven years, we moved to the more civilized center of town. Being twelve, and growing up, we were also ready to move on from the swamp to bigger and better adventures.

THE CANOE

My earliest memory is my mother putting me to bed in my crib with a nice warm bottle of milk, tucking me in, giving me a kiss and then closing the bedroom door. It did not take long after that for my older brother, remember we shared a room, to climb out of his crib into mine, chug a lug my milk and escape back to his crib. As you might imagine this didn't set too well with me and because I couldn't talk, my only recourse was to scream my head off. This of course drew my mother back into the bedroom to see what was wrong. She checked me out, took note that my bottle was empty, and then scolded me for making such a fuss. After several days of this routine, I finally realized that life wasn't fair and had to fight for what was mine. This is why in our household our meals resembled an eating contest with me and my brother fighting for the food. We sat quietly waiting for the meal prayer to be over, and then dove into the food like a couple of starving dogs. One day, to our great surprise, after our dinner eating contest was completed, my father informed us that he had ordered a canoe kit, which should arrive any day and my brother, Dad and I, were going to build a canoe.

This was really cool we both thought! After being Swamp Rats and having no means to travel over water, even trying to build rafts with little success, we lusted after the allure of having a boat. We got a little taste of how cool this would be when our family visited friends of theirs who moved into a new sub-division. They had a boy our age, and in the Swamp Rat tradition, we went out to explore. We soon discovered a creek and we had seen what looked like a little boat at a building site. We didn't quite know what this was, but it looked like it could float. It was about five feet long, a couple of feet wide, and about, eight inches or so high. Now, being the devilish kids that we were, it didn't take long for the call of the wild to beckon to us. We dragged our little boat to the creek, and with much joy, off we went. Our little boat didn't perform as well as we had hoped, probably because it really was for mixing mortar and was not designed for three kids to be floating down a creek. We only had makeshift paddles made out of a couple of pieces of two by fours that we had also stolen. The creek was clogged with lots of dead trees, making travel difficult, but we were having a blast and surprisingly traveled quite a distance before we spotted a big dead woodchuck on the side of the creek. Remember, we had fooled around with trapping in our Swamp and had skinned many a dead animal, with the smelliest being a rabbit, which was the first animal that we ever skinned. I can still vividly remember my dad, after we clubbed our first couple of rabbits and brought them home to eat, showing us how to skin them. He did the first rabbit and my brother and I did the second one. We made the first cut and both promptly threw up, but managed to complete the job. As Swamp Rats we always had pocket knives with us and we decided to skin this big woodchuck. I don't truly remember if it was me or my brother who started to skin but with the first cut it caused an Up Chuck because it had been sitting dead for a couple of days and the odor was horrendous even for us trained skinner Swamp Rats. We quickly killed that idea, and I think the smell acted like smelling salts and got us back to the real world making us realize that it was getting dark and we needed to get home. It did not take us long to figure out that traveling down stream was a lot easier than trying to go up stream. We did the logical kid thing, sunk the boat for future use, and followed the creek back to the friend's house. I bet this mystery really freaked out the bricklayer who found his motor mixing tub gone and nowhere to be found. I wonder to this day if anyone ever found our little boat that we never saw again. When we arrived at our friends' house, our parents weren't surprised at all at our completely filthy condition. They hosed us off outside, then made us strip down naked, hosed us again, got some towels and friend's clothes, and we were good to go. This was the usual routine for us kids but not something you'd see in today's world.

We waited impatiently, for what seemed like forever, for our canoe kit to arrive and finally it came. It came in several really big boxes and the wonder of turning this into a canoe began. Our house was an old Tudor design with a closed in porch that was heated and used as a family room. Our Dad, to my mom's much objection, decided to build the canoe on the porch. What a trip, we were going from our little short mortar tub to this canoe, which was going to be18' 2" long and 39" wide. We didn't know squat then about canoes, but realize now that this was a really big canoe. In addition, we had no clue what a big project this was going to be.

We all jumped in with great enthusiasm to begin this large project. The basic design of this canoe was a frame, ribs, keel, and gunnels, all built out of mahogany, and covered by panels made from thin marine plywood. First, we laid out a couple of sawhorses and started to lay out all the ribs and keel. All went pretty well until we started to put the skin panels on. This proved to be difficult, because they were hard to bend, and very time consuming with the number of screws we had to put in. Soon my brother and dad lost interest, but I doggedly continued. My guess, this challenge to finish the canoe, was the beginning of my love affair with canoes, and I remember, not unkindly, of working many hours on the canoe by myself.

Finally, after what seemed like forever as a twelve-year-old kid, the canoe was finished. Now it was time to take the canoe out of the porch and into the water. *UH! OH!* A slight miscalculation; the canoe was too big to fit through the windows on the porch. What are we going to do now? After much argument between my dad and mom, my mom agreed to the only solution. Take the windows out. That did the trick and the canoe was free.

The DuPage River was close and we immediately made plans to get our prize into the water. There was a park nearby that we could use to launch the canoe into the river. Oops! How do we get this very big thing there? More thought, and help from my dad's work buddy, who had a rack and a with a mile of rope. We finally got it semi secured on dad's car and off we went to canoe the mighty DuPage River. I can remember, as if it was yesterday, how great it was when I first got into the canoe. It actually floated, was stable, and paddled easily. *"How cool this wasn't even close to that tub on the creek."* I thought. The love was consummated!

Now I am a canoe instructor and guide and love to build things. I love to fish, bow hunt, gun hunt, camp, and canoe and know I how to finish even the hardest projects. These were gifts that my dad gave me and makes me love and miss him even more today.

The many things my dad exposed me to helped me become the person that I am today. I hope all you parents out there realize how important it is to share your passions with your kids and not follow only the whims of our society. I fear that this is not happening in the modern family, and is a big injustice to the children of our time. Last, but not the least, if you want excellent memories you have to have excellent adventures!

FREEDOM-DUMB OR NOT?

We paddled the DuPage River several times over the next several years. As we got older, it became clear that more adventure was in order. Before I impart this next story, I must set the stage of what kind of shenanigans we kids were up too by age sixteen.

We graduated from our BB guns to pellet guns and were hard pressed to shoot much in town, which was a real bummer since we were used to the freedom of the Swamp. One of the ways we alleviated this problem was to sit on our back porch and take pot shots at birds. We had a long skinny lot, which was bordered by a lot of trees, and offered a good degree of privacy. Don't get to upset now, because we did have some rules. No robins, blue jays, cardinals, or any other songbirds. Everything else like black birds etc. was free game.

I think one of the prerequisites, before buying a house, is to have a sit down with your neighbors. There is nothing worse than having a bad one. Well, we did! Our neighbors to the north were a bitter couple without kids who would complain about everything that we kids did. They installed a high fence but still snooped on us.

My friend Gary and I were happily plinking at birds with the pellet gun on our secluded porch, when low and behold a cop was at our door and proceeded to haul us down to the station, because said neighbor called and complained. Of course, my parents weren't home because they wouldn't have approved of us shooting from the back porch. This particular cop was notorious, in our kid world, for his over reaction to situations. The most famous was when he drew down on some kids at the local movie theater for not keeping quiet. Along with my dad, who looked like Barney Fife, this local cop was another image of Barney Fife from the Andy Griffith Show. For those of you who may be too young to remember the Andy Griffith Show, it was about a small town in the mountains of the South. Andy Griffith was the Sheriff and Barney Fife was the screw up Deputy, who was allowed only one bullet, which he had to keep in his pocket. Our local Barney Fife took Gary and I down to the basement of the police station, which was all cement walls and ceiling. He then proceeded to read us the riot act. He said, *"These pellet guns are as powerful as a 22 and you have to be careful with them"* and so on. All this stuff we already knew, being well versed in the use of kid's weapons. Then Barney, the local cop, to our great surprise, took the gun walked to the corner of the room and fired.

Gary and I immediately hit the floor. As I said, we knew how powerful the gun was and were not as stupid as the cops thought. As the pellet was ricocheting around the room, it hit Barney's partner in the arm. The shot partner started to scream, *"What the f**** you stupid A**"* *and* so on. He was not a happy camper. Gary and I were busting a gut trying not to laugh our heads off. The partner took Barney upstairs continuing with his tirade. Well, after that fiasco, the only way to save face was to let us go. There was no law anyway forbidding the use of BB guns and Pellet guns in town, but we didn't push that point.

My good friend Andy, who I met almost immediately upon moving into the neighborhood at age twelve, lived a couple of doors down, and we have hung together ever since. He had a Granddad, who had a wee bit of a problem with alcohol, who would buy us booze if we gave him money so he could buy booze also.

Andy and I hung with a gang of about six and one older co-worker was twenty-one, and had a house that was not far away. I made friends with him at age fifteen while we were working together at Dog and Suds. Soon after I met Co-worker Ralph, I introduced him to my other friends, and we planned a party for all of us and our co workers at Dog and Suds. I really wanted to go but knew there would be no way my dad would allow me to attend. It was going to start after work at about midnight and they said they would pick me up. My brother Bruce had his own room on the first floor of our house and I shared a room with my baby brother Matt upstairs next to my parents' room. Bruce would routinely go out his window at night after our parents would go to bed and do his own shenanigans and never got caught. Sorry again Bro!

It was summer time and hot, and I thought I would try the same scheme by saying I was hot and was going to sleep on the porch to beat the heat. I had arranged to be picked up a little before midnight and snuck out when they arrived and went to the party. After about an hour of hard partying, there was a knock on the door and whom do you think showed up. I bet you can guess, my very angry dad who had found out by calling a co-worker's dad son who grilled him hard and he squealed on me. My dad must not have been impressed with my story and checked the porch, or maybe he just got up to go the bathroom downstairs and found the bed empty. Of course, my squealing friend was not a former swamp rat who would never have talked even under the intense grilling of their parents. There was a big embarrassing scene. I was dragged off home, big fight, including blows thrown, then escape and on the lamb. My friend's house was in the country on the edge of town a couple of miles away. I traveled in the bushes out of sight; sure, that I was going to be nabbed by the police and made my way back to the party. Ralph welcomed me with open arms, and I stayed the night. The whole time I was thinking, *"I had really done it now, soon I was going to be carted off to jail."* To my great surprise the next morning, my mom and dad showed up at the door. And were not angry but apologetic and worried that I would really run away for good, which stupidly I was considering. Ralph let them in; we talked, made up and went home.

My dad was a great dad but had trouble extending the leash with a little trust as we kids grew up. This created the extreme friction that was between us. And now realize that this balance is a very hard thing to achieve. That night, I believe, he learned a lesson and gave us a little more leeway but not that much. Looking back at those times I realize the strict reality we had to live by, which we did not like, gave us the paranoia that we needed, not to step over the line and do something real stupid, which may have had life changing or ending consequences. On the other hand, when I got to college and had complete freedom, I went completely wild which was not good either. Hence, this is a hard balance to achieve. Bottom line is my dad probably saved my life a hundred times!

FIVE MEN IN A TUB

The above should set the stage for our first real canoe trip, excluding the mortar mix tub, down a river. Gary, Andy, Chris, George and me, yes that's right, five men in a tub, planned a canoe trip down another section of the DuPage River one nice Saturday morning. We did not know anything about this section of river and did not even know if the canoe could handle all five of us. Good thing it was a really big canoe, because we also had to have our cooler of beer.

My dad was well aware of this adventure because he did the shuttle for us and knew what we had planned. He even helped us get the canoe on top of Andy's car with our new Sears car top canoe suction cup rack and a half mile of rope. We should not have been surprised, and really were not, as to what was to transpire. We loaded everything, (we had already secretly loaded the cooler with beer in the trunk of Andy's car) and drove to our planned end point. And left Andy's car there and my dad drove us to our put in place, which is called a shuttle. We had lots of experience being sneaky about hiding booze. Our really big canoe was maxed out with five boys and a cooler full of beer. What we did not plan on was the number of trees across the river. We learned that day that when a boat is overloaded it becomes very unstable. I think the beer did not help either.

We soon became very efficient at righting a capsized boat and maneuvering around and over the many trees in the water. We did not mind this much, because of the beer and the excellent adventure we were having. We had a feeling; we knew how sneaky my dad could be when trying to catch us with the booze. Once again, imagine Barney Fife, my dad, lurking in the weeds as we went under a bridge, and us drunken kids pretending we were perfectly fine, being perfectly blasted, and not knowing that he was there. After a few bridges, he gave up and I am sure admonished himself for not trusting us kids. *"Sorry about that dad!"*

Now in retrospect, I wish he had continued to check on us, because George had grown weary of continually getting out of the boat and was now pulling the canoe along to minimize capsizes and facilitate travel. He was without shoes, which he lost in the mud, and we were making good time with this technique in our state (high) and the state of the river. We were teenagers and teenagers do not have much wisdom. The wisdom of walking in a river with no shoes, with who knows what is on its bottom, was not present. George stepped on something, not good, and got a very nasty cut on his foot. This sobered us up quickly as he was bleeding like a stuck pig and luckily, we were not far from our take out or he may have bled to death. A trip to the ER ensued with a bunch of stitches for George.

After the trip, we decided that we had learned a few things. First, we agreed we had a most excellent adventure. Second, it is smart to be paranoid of one's elders, although sometimes they can be reasonable, and we could use their help. Third, we learned it is smart not to walk in the river without shoes and to always wear shoes that will stay on your feet even in mud. Last, but not the least, if you want to have great memories you have to have excellent adventures.

SPRING BREAK

I lived in a dorm my first year of college with about 50 other students, and got to know a lot of them well. A bunch of them were planning a trip down to Fort Lauderdale Florida during spring break, and asked me if I wanted to go. I told them that I would love to, but had a big mid term test the day after they were leaving. They said that they couldn't wait but if I got down there, they would have a place for me to stay and a ride back. I really wanted to go, but *"how the heck was I going to get down there?"* I thought. I didn't even have a way to get home and was planning on hitch hiking. Back in the 60s there was not the same bad karma given to hitch hiking that there is today, so that was not such an unreasonable plan, although it would be a first for me. I was a bit worried about my generally ratty musician look. I did not know it then but there was a plan that must have been kicking around in my sub conscious.

I saw all my friends off, took the test the next day, packed my bags and caught a ride with another student on my dorm floor heading east. Lombard, a suburb of Chicago, where I lived, was about 40 miles due east of Northern Illinois University in Dekalb. He took me as far as Rt. 47, about 15 miles, and then he had to head north. Like a bolt of lightning my subconscious blasted forward and I realized that fate may have led me to this very intersection. I had two suitcases, a medium weight wool coat, and about $150 dollars in my pocket. If I went south, it would lead me to Florida, and if I continued east, it would lead me home.

I believe that this is the moment when my true adventurous soul was born. I am all alone, never hitched hiked in my life, not prepared at all, and am contemplating hitch hiking to Florida about 1500 hundred miles away. I thought, "Are you nuts?" I decided to let fate make the decision for me. I would go either east or south depending on who offered me a ride first in either direction. It was not long before Bob, a nice farmer picked me up. He was headed south to Dwight, and as fate dictated, another excellent adventure began.

After I got in the car with Bob, I was surprised how happy I was, and knew that this was really what I wanted to do. When Bob dropped me off, a little south of Dwight on Rt. 47, the traffic was light and I started to walk, thinking it was going to be a long hike to Florida. The wisdom of taking two suitcases was a little lacking, I thought, as I drudged along. I finally got a ride from a semi-truck driver, which was another first for me, that was going to St. Louis. I was really on my way now with no turning back!

I got acquainted with country music, and life on the road as a long-haul trucker. We were making great time swapping stories and were getting close to St. Louis. The trucker said, *"I got to get off the expressway and head north soon, be careful in this neighbor hood it is not too great."* He let me out just before we were going to cross the mighty Mississippi and into Missouri. I thanked him, he wished me luck, and off he went.

Uh-oh! I thought, *"Is it illegal to hitch hike on an expressway!"* It was 10pm; I had to cross this bridge, which had about a foot of room to walk on the side, with two suitcases and so began to hoof it as quickly as I could. Soon a semi, which is only inches away, nearly blows me over the side to become fish bait in the Mississippi, prompts a rush of adrenalin and fear as another one is coming soon behind it. I then realize this is not idle

paranoia and begin running for my life, doing the 200-hundred-yard Mississippi bridge dash on a one-foot ledge, and just make it before the next semi comes blasting by. *"That was too close, something I don't want to repeat,"* I thought. I was sweating, tired and burnt from the adrenalin rush of near death, but strangely elated, when a young black local took mercy on me and picked me up. He exclaimed, *"What the heck is a stupid white hippie doing in this black neighborhood at 10:00 o'clock at night."* I told him that I was heading to Florida for a Spring break and asked him if there was a bus station anywhere close, and said *"I ain't no hippy I'm a musician."* He said, *"Right."* I figured I could take a ride somewhere overnight, recoup and catch some sleep. He said there was one close and took me there. I thanked him and went into the Bus station. I went to the counter and inquired when the next bus was heading south. I was in luck. There was a bus to Memphis leaving in a couple hours and it cost only $22.00. *"Whew, I thought I can get some shut eye before the bus arrives."* Nope, a cop at the bus terminal would prevent you from sleeping by whacking you in the leg with his baton. I guess this was to discourage any vagrants from sleeping at the station. I told him, *"I had a ticket and was waiting for a bus and was no vagrant. I was a musician."* But he whacked me anyway. I guess he didn't like musician types that looked like hippies.

The bus left about midnight and life was good. I was lucky to have two seats to myself. I don't think anyone wanted to sit next to a ratty looking musician, and I got some good Z's. *"There is a positive side to looking a little ratty,"* I thought. We arrived in Memphis at

5:30am in the middle of the city, in another bad neighborhood. Good thing I thought, *"it's early, nobody is up yet"* and the race was on. My two suitcases and I set an Olympic record for the fastest two-suitcase race out of town. *"My second Olympic record"* I thought. The town started to wake up as I raced through the city, trying to hitch hike as I ran with no luck and hoofed it all the way out. Once I got a little away from the city I got a ride with a nice man, a little too nice. He informed me that he was gay, and I informed him that I was not and we got along just fine. We were heading generally toward Atlanta, which I figured might be a place I could repeat what I did last night, and grab a bus to get a little shuteye. My new gay friend and I talked up a storm about the prejudices of our times and how screwed up the world was. I was well versed in these subjects and then I realized maybe I was a hippy after all! He let me out when he had to go in the wrong direction, wished me luck and I thanked him. I was picked up soon, by my first real hillbilly, who was mortified that a hippy was hitch hiking in the south and he felt sorry for me. What a change I thought. *"Gay man to red neck, maybe my hippie look was not such a detriment,"* I thought. I had learned that my job as a hitchhiker was to provide some entertainment, which so far seemed to be one of the reasons, along with curiosity about a young hippy looking guy caring two suitcases, that people would pick me up. The gay guy may have had other intentions, which I could understand, because I would have picked up a girl, but he was a gentleman like I would have been. I also knew that the suitcases that were a hassle to carry, also made people feel sorry for me. I entertained all of them with stories of my excellent adventures, and had fun meeting all the different types of people. I had already learned that the people who picked me up were a lot more scared of me than I was of them. They would start the conversation with, *"you are not going to hurt me are you"?* I would reply *"Of course not. I am just a student on Spring break on my way to Florida to meet friends from school and have some fun"* That would break the ice and lots of interesting conversation would begin. The biggest lesson that I was learning is that most people are very nice. We are all bombarded with bad news about bad people all the time by the media. I think this has given us all a warped view of the world and make people overly paranoid, and was happy I was learning different.

I was getting close to my destination of Atlanta and the next driver was about my age and said he would take me close to Atlanta. He had a little smoke, which, to be friendly I partook. It was not long before we were at his friend's house partying hardy.

Sometimes life is just too good. Now, after an afternoon of partying and a good buzz, he followed through with his promise and got me to the outskirts of Atlanta. He also warned me about the general dislike of hippies because of the Anti-war movement that was going on. I told him I looked like a hippie but was only a peace-loving musician. He said,

"*Right.*"

I knew I had to catch a ride outside of the city because I already knew, hitch hiking in the city sucks. It was early evening now and I lucked out and found a ride into the city, and again I was warned about the general attitude toward hippie types, and now was tired of explaining about the musician thing. He told me, when he let me out, that I was about 20 blocks from the bus station and I began to walk.

I had not taken the warnings seriously, because everyone had been so nice. Suddenly a man screams out his window. *"Commie Fagot, Hippy Traitor, get a haircut."* I was right in the middle of Atlanta and other people were rolling their windows down and screaming all manner of bad things. *"Not Good"!* I thought. My buzz had worn off and quickly decided it was time now for me and my suitcases to go into high gear and ran for my life setting a new scared shitless two suitcase Olympic dash record in the middle of a right-wing dick wad city. It was a sobering, literally, experience and I now knew what real prejudice felt like. It sucks! Something nobody should have to endure.

"Thank God, I made it," I thought as I got to the station. I went to the ticket window and inquired again about overnight and found I could ride to Jacksonville for $20 bucks and life was good again. I was even able to get some shuteye in this station, which was a surprise in this right-wing dick wad city I was sure there would be a Nazi cop with a club at the station. The bus left at 12:30am and would arrive again in the early morning, which I thought was great, because it probably was also in a bad neighborhood and I did not need any more hassle.

I went to sleep, and slept soundly, waking up in Florida. Hooray! Life on the road was now becoming routine and again had to walk out of Jacksonville trying this time to be more relaxed, because it could not be as bad as it was in Atlanta and it seemed that the people in the bad neighborhoods were a lot nicer than the people who were in the nice neighborhoods, like in Atlanta. This really proved to be true in Jacksonville and I was soon out of the city. I was not having much luck hitch hiking yet, but was enjoying the beautiful cloudless morning, reveling in the warmth, when suddenly a Volkswagen passes me and slams on its breaks. I ran up to the car and could not believe what I'm looking at. It was kids from my dorm who were also going to Ft. Lauderdale and they recognized me. *"Unbelievable"* I shouted in glee. What great luck, these were not the friends who had invited me, but I knew I should be able to find them in Lauderdale, wherever the most girls where.

The rest of this story is what you would expect. I shared a room the first night at their hotel with my dorm friends and the next day to their great surprise, I found my other dorm buddies on the beach of course surrounded by babes, who were staying with relatives that lived in Ft. Lauderdale. The rest of the trip was partying; girls, sunburn, and a crowded ride back in a nice big boat of a car and back to college.

I learned many things on this trip. First, this was my first truly solo adventure where I was completely on my own. It came in a flash of inspiration that I believe has shaped the rest of my life. I conquered my fears and followed my heart, and had an excellent adventure. The pressures of society and one's fears often dissuade people from following their dreams. This trip, I believe, was the beginning of my gaining the wisdom of following your dreams. And along with what I learned from performing as a musician helped me have the self-esteem to make these dreams a success. Second, most people are nice, and the nicest were the poorest. Third, some people are real prejudice dick wads, and know now, how much it sucks. Fourth, sleeping on buses is a good way to go, and bus travel is cool. Fifth, walking with suitcases is a bummer but helps you get rides. Sixth, life is stranger than fiction. Last but not the least, if you want to have great memories you have to have excellent adventures.

COLLEGE BUDDIES, BATS, AND FLOOD

In college, I hung around with three guys who lived on the same dorm floor with me. We did way too much partying, which shouldn't surprise you. We were like a bunch of wild monkeys let out of a cage. To all you parents out there, it may be good advice to give your kids a little freedom before college, maybe getting some of the just freed monkey out of them. One time, I came back from class and to my great shock, found my side of the dorm room, that I shared with a roommate, completely empty. I mean furniture and all; there was not even a scrap of paper left, just a lot of nothing. My roommate was a very straight farm boy, he wouldn't even look at the posters of nudes that a normal teenager full of hormones, had on my side of the room. He had been in a high school bus that was hit by a tornado and a bunch of kids got killed. The sound of thunder gave him a panic attack. So, I figured he was not the perpetrator. The other weird thing about him was that he brought a pet chicken to college with him. I guess that was a farmer thing, or maybe the idea was to calm him down with a little piece of home. He only made it a semester and to my chagrin, one day all his stuff was gone and except for the damn chicken. Well, there are only two things a chicken is good for, one, is to lay eggs which this one didn't do because he was a rooster, and second is to eat. They make lousy pets. I, on the other hand knew who was behind the phenomena of missing everything. My whacked out, also just freed monkey dorm buddies, Billy, Bill, and Rich. Off I went with purpose in search of my buddies and all my stuff. I found my buddies and threatened their collective devious lives and they finally gave it up. My stuff was crammed on one of the elevators. They helped me restore my life back to normal after they had a great laugh, while I was silently planning my revenge. After the appropriate cooling off time, I rigged their dorm room door with a garbage can filled with water to drop on their heads when they opened their door. What is that saying, who laughs first laughs last? That's not right. Who laughs last, laughs first? Anyway, I got the last laugh!

I took the next semester off to play a couple of months with a band I was with, at a Playboy Club in Lake Geneva Wisconsin. Can't blame a nineteen-year-old who has dreams of that, but remained friends with my dorm buddies. Rich, was from Quincy Illinois and Bill, Billy and I decided, that summer, to take a road trip to visit him. So, off we went. We did the usual stuff, partying, but of course, we were up for some adventure also. Richard informed us that he knew of a wild cave that we could go and explore. We scrounged up some flashlights and off we went. It was hard to find in a surprisingly wild country. *"Perfect"* I thought. We found a path that Rich said should take us to the cave. We had to jump a small creek, and were soon at the mouth of the cave up the side of a large bluff.

Caves are made from water seeping down from a bluff, made out of limestone, making tunnels and caverns. The opening wasn't very large and we slithered in and proceeded to get scared shitless as a bunch of bats blasted out. We soon climbed down and made it to a large cavern, which was quite cool, and continued to have a blast exploring the cave for a good three hours, before returning to the entrance, tired and muddy. To our great dismay, it was pouring out! We were already wet form the cave and decided to blast back to our vehicle about a mile away and off we went.

We soon hit the little creek, which was now a raging torrent. All our mouths fell open in complete surprise, and exclaimed in unison, *"Oh F****!"* The creek was about 20 feet across with big waves and a powerful current. This was my first, and little did I know not my last, experience with flash floods. All of us were strong swimmers, but none of us would brave these waters. We were dumb, but not that dumb to jump in this raging torrent. I said, *"There must be a way around the creek."* Rich said, *"I think that is our only choice."* We then headed, which we thought was straight North, in this very wild and over grown terrain. Our progress was not good. We beat around for a while and soon again came to the river. *"Not good!"* Billy cried. We followed the river back to where we started, went the other direction, and again came to the river. We cried, *"Shit!"* Luckily it had stopped raining but it was getting late and we were starting to get a little worried. We then decided to go back to the cave and try going in the opposite direction. Again, we came to the raging river. *"We're surrounded"* Bill said. We were getting frustrated and even more tired and cold and came to an old dilapidated house, and debated staying the night. Rich said,*" We have no beer."* We were all wet, cold, tired and hungry and most importantly, we had no BEER! *"Let's try one last time and if we are not successful then we will stay the night,"* I declared. It wasn't hard to find the raging river again, because no matter which way we went we ran into it. Once we found it, we followed it back to where we thought we came from. Then I spied a tree that was three quarters across river. The tree was at a bend and it looked like if I shimmied out on the tree and then took the plunge it should push me into the far bank. We were desperate at this point. I said, *"I think if I shimmied my way out carefully to the end of the tree and dropped into the river, I think it will push me into the bank on the far side."* Bill said, *"What are you nuts?"* I replied, *"Probably, but remember we have no beer."* Bill said, *"Good*

Luck." I shimmied out carefully and dropped in. It was shockingly cold and it blasted me to the opposite shore into a nice eddy and I was across. My friends followed and we were free. "*Hooray*" we all shouted! It wasn't long before we got back to the car. OH! I forgot we had already been chanting "*CHEESEBURGERS, ChEESEBURGERS, BEER, BEER*" and immediately went for cheeseburgers and beer as soon as we got back to civilization.

One of the things I have learned, as a guide and canoe instructor over the years, is a very effective self-rescue technique, which we really could have used that day trapped by the flash flood. You can cross a ragging river or whitewater by using the current to help you and not fight it. To do this you swim, using the breast stoke at an angle to the current so it hits you on one side, which then pushes you the opposite way. If the current is hitting you on your right side, the current will push you to the left. You will move very quickly if you find the right angle. You must always be aware if you try this of the possibility of going into a downed tree, which we call a strainer, because if you do go into one, it may suck you down and you can drown even with a life jacket on. We use this technique a lot in whitewater canoeing to cross rivers and it is called a forward ferry. Do not try this unless you have been trained, or the as a last resort for survival. Always be very cautious of fast running water and always wear your lifejacket.

We all thought that this was an excellent adventure and had a great party to prove it, and again decided we had learned a couple of good lessons from our adventure. First, where there are caves the possibility of flash flooding is strong. Second, we should have checked the weather report. Third, bringing a map to find an escape route would have been wise. Fourth, a compass would have been a good idea. Fifth, bring extra dry warm clothes, and some food. Last, but not the least, if you want to have great memories you have to have excellent adventures.

THE FIRST CANADIAN TRIPS (THE LEARNING PROCESS)

The first trip to Canada was an impromptu trip with my brother Bruce. Bruce had just finished college and had some free time. I was a musician and out of work now with nothing to do, so off we went. We grabbed our only tent, a canvas two-man pup tent from our Indian Guide days that my dad had bought, some very crude cook gear, (not much), fishing stuff and did not take our canoe, because my brother did not want to put it on his car. We went into Canada, with no plan, and ended up in a semi-wild place north of Toronto, where we could rent an aluminum canoe and do a couple of nights camping and a day of fishing. We paddled out on the large lake and found a place to camp. We set our little pup tent, put in our not so good ground pads and sleeping bags. And made a concoction of macaroni, cheese, and tuna fish for dinner. We had a nice night sitting around the fire and were amazed at how many stars we could see. The next morning, we got up, had some cereal, instant coffee, and got ready for a day of fabulous fishing.

We got in the canoe and proceeded on our quest to catch fish. We had little luck, probably because we did not have a clue about how to fish a large Canadian lake. We knew from our map that we could portage into another small lake. And figured it should be less fished and easier to fish in a canoe making the decision easy. We found the portage trail and did not have a clue about how to portage a canoe, but we managed trying several different ways to carry a canoe and even tried the just drag the sucker method. It was a lot longer than we anticipated, but we were young, strong, and fresh. We were correct in the assumption that a smaller lake is much easier to fish from a canoe. We soon found out that without wind we could stay in one place. And being smaller we were able to find some fish. *"Hooray!"* my brother shouted as he caught the first fish. We fished a long time and had a blast catching some pan fish. It was getting late so we began to head back. We decided not to keep any of the fish that we caught because we did not want carry them over the damn portage trail. And which now seemed like a monumental task and did not have a good way to cook them anyway. This also made the fish's day when we let them go. We were already tired when we arrived back at the portage trail and with dread in our hearts, we began to carry our canoe. It seemed to take forever and at the end, we only had the energy to revert to dragging our canoe over to the other side. To our great surprise, the wind had increased greatly, making whitecaps on the lake, and "OH NO"! I exclaimed "It's a f**** headwind. We discovered that day that paddling against a headwind was lots harder than normal paddling, and it took us until almost dark to paddle back to our campsite. We were completely exhausted, after our epic battle against the wind, when we arrived back. To make matters worse, luckily after a tasty dinner of hot dogs and beans, it started to rain. We quickly escaped to our tent to crash for the night and quickly found out that if you touch any part of a canvas tent while it is raining the water will wick right through and into the tent. *"Not Good!"*, I said. My brother replied, *"You Think."* The tent was small, not touching the sides proved to be a real problem, but exhaustion soon won out and we slept like logs, or more like a couple of wet dogs.

The next day was nice, sunny and calm, so we bugged out quickly and headed back to the resort café for some… Guess what? Cheeseburgers and beer, and headed for home.

We learned a lot from this first attempt at a canoe trip. First, big lakes are hard to fish in a canoe. Second, smaller lakes are much better to fish in a canoe. Third, portages are a bitch. Fourth, wind on a lake is a bigger bitch. Fifth, canvas tents suck. Last but not the least, if you want to have great memories you have to have excellent adventures.

SECOND CANADIAN TRIP (TRASH MOBILE)

The next Canadian Trip was with my friend Andy. Andy has a great mellow personality, loves the outdoors, and most importantly loves an excellent adventure. When things get tough Andy is the guy to be with, and over the years of excellent adventures this was proved over and over again, which you will hear about soon.

The first car I owned was a 53 Dodge that was on its last legs, for $50. I think it lasted all of four months until it gave up the ghost. My dad helped me find a nice 1964 Chevy Impala that had only 60,000 miles for $300 dollars. This was in 1969 and I was 19 years old. And was a great car that I drove for 100,000 more miles, which we named the Trash Mobile. You can probably figure out why.

Learning from the first Canadian trip, which I had told Andy about in detail, we tried to make some improvements in our gear. Andy said, *"My cousin has a nylon tent that should be more waterproof than your canvas tent."* I said, *"Cool, now we need to pack more cooking equipment so we can actually cook something"* And proceeded to fill a large duffle bag, about four feet tall, with all manner of pots and pans, and said, *"That should do it."* We packed a big Colman stove, one of those that you had to pump, and a gallon of Colman fuel, a five-horse outboard motor, a canoe motor mount, five-gallons of gas, a large cooler, lots of clothes, fishing stuff and all manner of other stuff. Needless to say, in order to fit this all in the car, even with the large trunk the Trash Mobile had, we had to remove the back seat, after clearing away of course some of the trash. This time we did take the canoe and were proud at getting better at tying it down, only using an eighth mile of rope. We congratulated ourselves, with high fives, for thinking of everything after being so unprepared on my first Canadian trip. *"Let's see I said,"* waterproof tent, adequate cook gear, big stove and hopefully enough fuel for trip, lots of food, and we are not going to get tired fighting the wind with the motor, lots of clothes, all our fishing gear and an adequate (huge) supply of beer and booze. *"Sounds about right,"* Andy said. *"Don't know if we got enough booze, but we can always buy more"* I mused.

The half hour machine was invented on this trip. I bet you are thinking, what the heck is that? Well, it's actually quite cool, but some of the techniques we employed, you may want to alter for safeties sake and the possibility of being arrested. We were still foolish kids at heart having a taste for alcohol. And were not averse to having a few cocktails while driving. I'm mortified now and certainly wouldn't do it or recommend it to anyone, but what can I say, we were devilish young adults. Alcohol, as you may have figured out, was a big part of our social structure. We had a high tolerance for alcohol, because we drank so much, and would make roadies as we traveled, which we thought was a big part of the half hour machine. And now realize, because we don't drink and drive anymore, it is not what makes the half hour machine work.

The whole premise behind the half hour machine is our perception of time always changes. When one is bored to tears say, in a boring lecture, waiting for someone, or at the dentist, time almost stands still. The opposite is true when you are at a party having fun with a buzz going and are having a heated discussion about some interesting topics. So, we took this premise to the car and it worked great. It seemed like it took only a half

hour to get anywhere. Now, before you judge us, realize that people use the half hour machine a lot now, when they text or talk on a cell phone while driving, also a stupid idea. I think it has to be that half hour machine thing also but they just don't know what it is called. This is why my memory is shaky on car travel on these trips. It is the damn half hour machine's fault!

Our plan was to head to International Falls, go north of there, and find a good place to take a three or four-day trip. Planning was not high on our list back then. Everything was going well, we had a great half hour machine going, and the trash mobile was purring like a kitten. And then we hit the border! I always feel tension when I go through customs now because of some of my experiences there and this is the first one of them. I don't know why we were worried, because we didn't have anything, we thought to hide. But it just might have been, because we were buzzed and had been on the road for a couple of days without showers, in the trash mobile and maybe we looked a little like riff raff. Everyone was passing through with no trouble, until the dreaded words came out of the customs guy's mouth *"Please pull over there and get out of your vehicle." "Oh Shit,"* Andy exclaimed. He then proceeded to go through the car with literally a fine-tooth comb, which was incredible because of course this was the trash mobile and you know there was a reason for this name. We had been on the road for a couple of days, adding to the trash, and with his face only inches away from the floor, he picked through all of it. After finding nothing he told Andy and I to follow him. Andy said to me. *"You think they're about to arrest us?"* I said, *"Probably."* The customs guy took us into a room and said, *"Take all your clothes off boys." "Didn't see that coming I thought."* He went through all our stuff and even told us to bend over and spread our cheeks, which was a humiliating experience. I thought to myself, *"Bad idea dude we ain't bathed for a couple of days, but it serves you right."* Finally, with no good reason not to, they let us into Canada. "Hooray!" I thought.

We are now in Canada, celebrating with a roadie, and merrily continued north ending up at the English River area, just North of Kenora Ontario. We talked to some locals who told us about a nice trip that we could take. It started on a big lake with a nice island campsite at the outlet where we could hang and fish for a couple of days, and then continue from there for another couple of days down through lakes and a river to the next access point. *"Perfect"* we thought and asked them where we could get some maps! They directed us to a bait shop where we got some maps and of course, we asked them where we could get some beer and booze. In Canada, you have to go to the government run Provincial stores for beer and liquor, which he directed us to.

We got to the put-in, a nice landing at our large lake, with great clear skies and no wind. Loaded our mounds of gear that barely fit into our very large 18'3" canoe, put the five hp motor on the side, and almost started the trip by flipping over. *"We have to be careful with this much weight on the side of canoe,"* I yelled, and off we went. We found out right away, that the motor was a little too big for even our very wide and long canoe. And if we opened her up, water would go over the sides and into the canoe, even at half throttle we were flying along. I shouted at Andy over the roar of the motor *"Isn't this great!* He turned around to reply and oh boy, we almost went in the drink. I shouted back, *"Stay perfectly still or we're going to be swimming.*" He said, "*no shit Sherlock!*" We should have remembered how unstable the canoe was when we had the five of us in the canoe on the DuPage River where we dumped a bunch of times, but you know it takes a while sometimes for us young punks to learn. Our canoe was easily as loaded as that and even maybe a bit more. We traveled for a couple of anxiety-filled hours and found the great campsite the locals had talked about, on a nice island about two miles from the outlet of the lake and start of our trip.

It took us a while to set up camp with all the crap we had and managed to try a late day fish. The next day we spent fishing, drinking and eating, with no rain or wind, and decided, running out of beer and booze, that we needed a re-supply before the start of our trip the next day. We got up early, knowing we needed time for a trip, even with a motor, back to civilization. The weather was calm when we left in the morning, but started picking up a bit when we landed. We made great time and the boat was way more stable without the load. We spent a couple of hours shopping and were successful in getting all that we needed.

We bought a couple of cases of beer and a bottle of booze and when we arrived back at the landing, we were surprised at the big waves, complete with whitecaps on the lake. I thought, "*I'm glad we brought the motor, wouldn't like to paddle in this wind*" Then an elderly local who watched us load our boat, came up and said, "*It's a little rough out there today boys. Eh! Do ya thenk it wise to brave her?*" We were a little nervous but our canoe was big and stable don't ya know, we had a motor to fight the wind, and we were young and stupid and didn't follow much advice, and replied, "*We have a big boat, we should be fine*", and off we went. It did not take us long to become scared shitless, but no way were we going back to listen to the "I told you so" of that old Canadian. Then about half way across the dreaded happened. We swamped.

Good thing the canoe was big and wide and had a lot of natural flotation because we didn't flip over and we didn't sink, and the motor, which was still above water along with our heads didn't quit. I yelled at Andy the obvious *"Stay perfectly still or we'll lose her."* He said, *"No shit Sherlock!"* Luckily, we were only a couple hundred yards from an island, which we carefully motored to. But now I thought, *"Should have listened to that old guy."*

Freezing cold, we unloaded, emptied the canoe and bravely set off again. A sane person would have headed back to the landing, but again we were not going to face "the I told you so." We were smart enough to re-distribute the load and Andy rode sitting on the floor of the canoe, more in the middle. We were extremely cold, and still scared shitless making for a long anxiety filled trip. And finally made it back without incident. *"Thank God"* I thought.

We quickly changed clothes, made a fire, and got some good whiskey in the gullet. I guess we thought we had a good excuse. And drank half of all the booze and beer that night. The good news is that we only burned a few things drying them over the fire, which may have been a blessing with the large load that we had. And the bad news was waking up to astronomical hangovers. To make matters worse, it was still really windy and we had the rest of this big lake to travel. Most people would have given up the ghost right there, but not us. We are all about excellent adventures.

We loaded everything up and Andy rode on the floor of the canoe for stability, which we had learned from our nightmare of the day before. What we did not figure on, is the amount of weight we now had, with the mounds of gear in the canoe. It did not take us long to realize that we were in big trouble again, because our overloaded canoe was very unstable and soon took on water. Andy began bailing with a purpose and we both again were scared shitless. I was kind of like driving on a glare ice road but worse.

After another eternity, but which was only about an hour, we made it to the river where life got a lot better until we hit the portage!

Remember all the crap we had in the canoe. There was a cooler full of beer, a five-horse motor, five gallons of gas, a giant duffle bag of pots, including some cast iron ones, all the camp stuff, fishing stuff, clothes, fresh food and who knows what all. *"Good thing it is only about a ¼ mile,"* I said. Yeah Right! It took only five grueling trips, one of them being a hundred pounds plus canoe and over an hour later, we were over. *"Whew!"* I thought, *"Glad that's done for the day."* Yeah right, it wasn't long before another portage came along.

We continued on, after *"what the hell were we thinking bringing all this stuff"* was revolving in our heads. We came to a small creek, looked at our map and found that it led to a small lake. You would think, after the day that we had, that we would not be up for taking a side trip, which may include yet another portage and who knows what. But the allure of the wild and the possibility of great fishing took over and up the creek we went. The good news was we did have paddles! This is why I love Andy so much and why he is a great traveling companion because he is as crazy as I am and loves an excellent adventure. We got in late, struggled to find a camp, tired, and it was raining. We got everything set up, ate some food, don't remember what, except the tent was dry, and thought, *"Ain't this great"* and crashed.

The next morning, we got up to a beautiful sunny day, ate some breakfast, and took the empty canoe out on a small lake to try the fishing. Bang! First cast, a nice sized Pike. Bang! Second cast, a nicer Pike. Andy said *"Things are really looking up"*! I said, *"No shit Sherlock"* as I hauled in another good pike. We spent the day catching fish and the evening stuffing our faces and attempting to lighten our load by mass consumption of the remaining beer. Sometimes life is just too good!

We had a great dry night of sleeping and woke up again to a beautiful day. And only minor hangovers. It must have been all that fish we ate, and off we went. We are now paddling, because it is too shallow for the motor, with the current, no wind and making good time. *"This canoe trip thing is really turning into an excellent adventure,"* Andy yelled. We arrived at our take out just after lunch and our plan was to hitch hike back to our car. After sitting for a couple of long hours, without a half hour machine going, we both began to realize, but didn't want to state the obvious, that this might not have been such a great plan. We were in the wild and had not seen a soul in three days. This made for much speculation of the wisdom of this, and I exclaimed, *"I wonder how long it will take us to hoof the 40 miles back to the Trash Mobil."* Andy replied, *"probably about 3 days but how are we going to carry all our stuff?"* I said *"these flat feet are not made for walking,"* and we continued to wait for another couple of stress filled hours. All of a sudden, we spotted a pickup truck flying down the road toward us, *"please pick us up"* we prayed jumping up and down and waving our arms like crazy people. He took pity on us, probably thinking what the heck were these young punks doing in the middle of nowhere, and stopped. He said, *"Need a ride boys, eh?"* We jumped in and he blasted off like the cartoon roadrunner being chased by the dumb coyote. Isn't life grand we thought as our teeth were rattling and our bodies bouncing while the driver was bragging about the new shocks he just put on the truck. And flying down this extremely rough road shouting, *"Isn't the ride great, eh?"* Yeah Right! Now we thought, *"Thank God that this guy wanted to show off his new shocks to someone or we would still be sitting there."*

He dropped us off back at the landing where we had left the trash mobile, with a few loose teeth and our insides mixed up like a milk shake. We were ecstatic to be back and thanked him for the ride. We are now ready to travel back to the old USA and thought we had better tidy up the trash mobile a bit, not a small task, before going through customs at the US border. We started a major clean, and low and behold right where the Canadian customs guy had his face inches from the floor, there was a roach. Not that we never smoked pot before, but this was not a part of our traveling routine and wondered how in the heck it got there and how did he not see it. So of course, being law-abiding adults, we tossed the joint out. Yeah Right, and thanked our new wisdom that led us to clean the car and never again of course would we trust custom agents not to have planted a roach, to get us busted at the US border.

This trip took place about forty years ago and I don't remember much of the return trip. And must have been that damn half hour machine again! I know that we had no problems at the border or making it home. This goes to show you how important a good excellent adventure is. When you are in situations like those that we had on this trip, life becomes crystal clear. *"I need to take this seriously or I may not survive."* The joy one feels is indescribable when you do survive these intense situations and you are then truly alive and will never again take life for granted. We learned a lot of good lessons on this trip. One, try and look as normal as possible when crossing the border and also clean the car up well. Two, packing light is important for safety and hardship. Three, trust people who are older and have more wisdom. Four, don't trust customs officers. Five, go for it. And, last but not the least, if you want to have great memories you have to have excellent adventures.

THREE BAND MEMBERS AND A FRIEND

On my twenty-first birthday, and in need of some cash, Greg, a musician friend from high school whom I had been jamming with, and I, decided to start a band. He had an opportunity to get steady work at a gay bar in Chicago. First, before you jump to any conclusions, we are most definitely straight and I have been happily married for the last twenty-five years. Second, we were stone-broke! We threw together this band in a couple of weeks. Greg had a friend who was a banjo player and drummer who had somewhat of a rep in the area and I had a friend, who I played with all through high school, who was a bass player. I play keyboards and Greg plays Guitar. We went to try out for this gig with only a few songs to our name. We were young and did not know what to expect. We nervously put on our blues brothers' sunglasses for some mental protection and did the audition. They liked us, probably because they didn't have many choices, and we played there every other week for the next three months, and learned a lesson about judging people. They treated us very well and the band stayed together for the next six years. The whole career with the band and music could be another excellent adventure book, which I may pursue one day, but now let us get back on track with the canoe thing.

Dale, the bass player, Charlie, the drummer, Gary, friend of Charlie, and I decided to do a canoe trip in Canada. We headed for Sioux Saint Marie, crossed over the border and found the Mississagi River, which was in Southern Ontario on the east side of Lake Superior. We took Dale's van, friend Gary's car, my canoe, and Gary's canoe.

As you know, we learned a lot on the last trip, so we tried hard to pack light. We took a lot less cook gear and packed lighter food. We included macaroni and cheese with tuna, and more macaroni and cheese with pepperoni, peanut butter sandwiches, and pancakes. You see a theme here. We left the beer at home but not the whiskey. We also shared one tent, which saved some weight, and could distribute the weight between two canoes making each canoe lighter. This worked out great except for the X factor. The X factor was a couple of real good snorers. *"Maybe a couple of light two-man tents would have been better,"* I thought, after a sleepless night.

Because we drove two cars, the shuttle was no problem and a local outfitter gave us some information and a map on the trip. The Mississagi River flowed through typical Canadian Shield country, which consists of forest and granite outcrops ripped up by retreating glaciers during the ice age. The outfitter informed us that this trip had some whitewater on it, which would be a first for all of us. We loaded all our gear. Dale and I were in my big wooden canoe, and Charlie and Gary in his aluminum canoe. The river was very pretty flowing gently through the beautiful Canadian wilderness with no signs of any humans at all, when suddenly after a couple of hours of paddling, we see a beautiful manicured lawn with an old grisly Candian smoking a cigar and drinking a beer. He called out, "*Hey boys, want a beer, eh?*" I shouted back, "*Eh that sounds good.*" He proceeded to give us each a brew, which really hit the spot, and told us a story about the rapid that was only a mile ahead. He said, *"A couple of boys about year ago drown in that rapid. I saw them go by with no life jackets on. I yelled to be careful there was a good rapid coming up and it might be a good idea to put your life jackets on!"* They looked at me like I was a dumb old man and just laughed. Well, I guess the last laugh was

on me but it is a shame that those dump ass punks didn't listen to me." I know this story shook me up not having any experience with any whitewater. And when I looked round at my mates, I could see the fear in their eyes. We thanked our new Canadian friend for the beers and off we went, and yes, we put on our life jackets, which we had been sitting on. It was not long, before the theme from the movie Deliverance, played on banjos, was being nervously mimicked by all. Then Charlie said, "We *better go to shore to get some rocks to plug up are asses,*" we all laughed hysterically. For those who have not seen the movie let me explain. In the movie, there was a scene where a bunch of hill rods captured one of the paddlers and let's just say *"made him squeal like a pig."*

We soon heard the roar of the rapid and prepared to meet our maker. The technique, that we dumb novices employed, was crude, but it worked. We knew enough to paddle on opposite sides of the canoe to prevent a tip over. When two people are paddling on the upstream side of the canoe, they will soon be swimming. Smartly, we worked hard to prevent this by calling switches from one side to the next, with the stern, (rear) paddler ruddering to steer. We would paddle like trappers being chased by a bunch of rabid moose yelling, *"yahoo"* the whole way through the rapid. It seemed a lot harder than it was, but we had a blast. This dumb technique worked on this and the rest of the rapids on this trip because they were all milk runs. A milk run is a rapid where not much maneuvering is involved but the ride is good.

We found a good campsite the first night and being young, dumb and hungry, we ate a lot of the food that we brought. The second day I remember we saw our first moose, not rabid of course, but were scared nevertheless, in the wild, and ate just about all the rest our food. Oops, did not figure on that! Maybe we packed a little too light and obviously had no discipline at all.

The last day we got up, with only a few greasy pancakes with a little jelly to feed four big and hungry paddlers. "*UH! OH! NO FOOD and we have a long way to go!!*" Well, we boys were not used to going hungry and it didn't take long before our hunger became the main subject of our thoughts and conversation.

Dale and I were paddling in my large and wide kit canoe and Charlie and Gary were in a nice Grumman. They were fast and we were slow, which didn't matter on a river with a current, but then we hit the big lake and of course a dreaded strong headwind. Soon the chanting began. Cheeseburgers! Cheeseburgers! Cheeseburgers! This continued for the rest of a long hungry afternoon. You would have thought that we had been starving for a month. Just about when we thought we were all going to starve to death we spotted the landing. You would have thought that we had won the super bowl. There happened to be a food vendor at the resort where we landed and guess what they sold? "*CHEESEBURGERS! HEAVEN!*" We ate until we could eat no more. Lying on the grass, completely stuffed Charlie started relaying an erotic dream he had in the tent the night before.

Charlie said, "*I dreamt I walked into a clearing in the woods where there was this beautiful little doe. I looked into her beautiful big eyes and she looked right back at me with no fear. And to my surprise, began to shyly walk toward me and began to rub seductively against my legs,* "UH! OH! Better stop here. Freud would have a field day with this one. After a story like that, we quickly decided that we were up for heading home and back to our girlfriends and off we went.

We learned some more valuable lessons on this trip. First, packing light is great, but you can't eat all the food the first day! Second, find out who snores before the trip or bring sleeping pills or real good earplugs! Third, wide, long, and heavy boats are slow. Fourth, always plan for a headwind. Fifth, it would be a good idea to get your significant other into paddling, to avoid weird erotic dreams. Last, but not the least, if you want to have great memories you have to have excellent adventures.

BITING OFF MORE THAN YOU CAN CHEW

We did some other minor trips and now thought that we were hotshots with a canoe. So, Andy and I planned a grandiose trip. We decided to do the entire Bois Brule River, which runs north 44 miles in Northern Wisconsin, and into Lake Superior. We then planned to paddle east down the coast of Lake Superior, we figured another 40 miles, to the Apostle Islands. *"No sweat" we thought*! Andy had a 1968 Mustang convertible that was newer than the trash mobile so we decided to take it instead. The obvious problem was how to carry the canoe on a ragtop. Of course, you cannot. Andy had a boat trailer available because, being broke musicians, Dale and I were restoring the 1950 Carver Wood Boat for Andy's Dad in their garage on sawhorses, making the trailer available.

We soon discovered that a boat trailer is an easy way to transport a canoe, and with the White Whale, our big kit canoe now up right, made it a great place to transport gear. We weren't smart enough yet to wonder what would happen if it rained. We removed the back seat from the Mustang to make room for more stuff. I guess we still didn't have that light thing perfected yet, and off we went!

We got to the beginning of the Bois Brule with no incident, camped in the nice new four-man Eureka tent that Andy and I brought and planned to start our trip the next day. We did not have any way to do the shuttle, so again we thought that we would just wing it, and would try to hitch hike back. The next morning, we got up early, packed everything into the White Whale and off we went. We packed lighter now, but nothing to write home about, and still had a heavy load. The beginning of the river was beautiful marshland with little sign of humans. The current picked up during the day and we started to hit some little rapids. No sweat, we were having a blast and had that switch thing down. We camped that night at a great spot and continued on early the next morning. The rapids began to get a little harder and then one of them got a lot harder and BANG! We hit a sharp rock! UH! OH! Got a little crack in the front of the boat and it was leaking, but not too bad. "*Grea*t," we thought, continued, and soon camped. We were getting good at making concoctions out of different things for a tasty meal, had some libations, solved the world's problems around a nice fire, and crashed in our nice new tent. The next morning things were going great and mood was high until we hit Lenroot Ledges, which is a series of ledges, with not much room between each drop. To make matters worse, once you made one chute you had to try and cross the current to the other side of the river to make the next chute. This is not hard if you are trained, which of course we were most definitely not! You may recall, when we had to jump in the raging river that had trapped us, I talked about ferrying. This would be a great place to utilize this technique. You simply would make the first chute then back paddle stopping yourself and pitching the canoe with the back end facing the way you want to go. The current will hit the side of the canoe and push you sideways. The trick is to have just the right angle and right amount of effort in the back paddling. Unfortunately, we were not the hot shots we thought we were and soon crashed. Not knowing what to do, we walked the canoe down the chutes. Andy would be front and I would be in the back. It was very hairy and scary and we were banging the heck out of the canoe. *"Not good,"* I thought. We made it to the end by some miracle and thanked the heavens for our survival! With an emphatic *"OH Shit, the canoe is leaking like a sieve,"* Andy exclaimed, when he checked our crack! "Now *what?*" I asked. Being young and dumb, we had no repair materials at all, so our only choice was to abort the trip. What a bummer. We had only made it a little over two days.

Dejected we began to hitch hike back to the car. No luck, *"Crap,"* I said. We then started to walk and suddenly, Andy spied a big inner tube. We knew that the river is tubed a lot, took note of where it was, and decided, if it was still there when we returned with the car, it would be free game. We walked, what we thought was like forever, and finally got a ride back to our car. We stopped on the way back, picked up the inner tube, and were soon, back to our gear.

Here's that choices thing again. We knew that the biggest rapid on the trip was Mays rapid, which was just a little way down river of where we landed. We were bummed about aborting the trip and were still up for some adventure. So, we loaded all our gear and took the big inner tube, and we both climbed onboard and locked our arms back-to-back. Soon we heard the roar of the rapids, which turned out to be more of a fall. Laughing like a couple of hyenas in a banana tree, we were having a grand old time. Then we hit the falls and over we went. I hit forward and Andy hit backward. It was like being in a washing machine filled with a bunch of rocks and instantly we were fighting for our lives. We finally ended up in an eddy in about two feet of water, shocked but happy to be alive. My right thigh was killing me where the initial hit took place, and I thought it might be broken. I looked for Andy who was pulling his shirt up and made one of the classic statements of all time, *"Do ya see any ketchup coming from my back,"* he exclaimed! We helped each other and struggled out of the water.

We were beat up bad but we didn't think we had any broken bones. We learned some more important lesson so far on this trip. First, have a tougher canoe that can take a beating. Second, do a little more research about the river you are paddling, and have a plan that maybe you have an outside chance to complete. Three, our canoe skills could use a little work, no a lot of work. Four, two people on a tubing tube is a lot of fun before you hit the falls then - a real bad idea. Four, luckily, our bones are tougher than we thought. Last, but not the least, if you want to have great memories you have to have excellent adventures.

MELLEN

We were beat up bad, and had about ten days left of our vacation and wondered what to do. I said, *"What do you think Andy? We have a broken canoe and we're in no shape to paddle anyway; do ya think we should call Billy up and head there early for some R&R?"* He said, *"Sounds good! I'm a hurting puppy and cold beer and cheeseburger sounds great,* I replied. *"We can probably get a cheeseburger at his place. I know they serve food. I'll ask him when we call."*

I had a friend in College, Billy, as you should remember, whose parents bought a tavern in Mellen Wisconsin. Mellen is located in Ashland County and it was not very far from the Bois Brule. We were planning to visit Billy, who was expecting us but not this early. He said that his folks owned about 100 acres of woods that bordered National Forest land and had a great place to camp. We found a phone and let him know of the change of plans, grabbed a beer and headed to Mellen for a couple days of R and R and more importantly some healing.

We arrived in Mellen and saw that it was a typical Northwood's small town, and easily found Bill's family bar. It was a large two-story structure with a restaurant and bar on bottom and an apartment on top. It was older and in need of a paint job, typical of what you might expect in an older Northwood's tavern to look like. We entered, beat up and tired, during a busy dinner hour going on around us. The bar looked better from the inside with nice weathered wood floors and an old-time large bar. Billy was tending bar and greeted us with a smile and a nice cold beer and of course, we ordered our cheeseburgers right away. It was evident that this was the happening place in town.

Now, enough about small towns, but this will be relevant latter. The alcohol part we had down pat so we jumped right in. We got blasted, maybe because we hurt so bad or maybe because we felt out of place and probably because of all the above. At who knows how late, we made our way to our campsite on Billy's parent's 100-acre woods.

The sound of some large barking dogs woke me up, late the next morning. *"What the heck I thought in my hung over cloud."* When I looked outside, I saw the meanest looking dogs I had ever seen. That set an adrenaline rush through my body and cleared my head, not knowing what to do. With a sigh of relief, I then saw Billy who said *"whatever you do don't come outside, these are trained attack dogs and they can kill!"* "Great," I thought, *"I have an astronomical hangover, my leg hurts like hell and it had a spectacular array of impressive colors and now are we going to get killed by these dogs from hell?"* At that point, Andy woke up, looked at my leg and commented on the extent of my injuries, "Nice *leg eh!*" He then proceeded to show me his back and said, *"Take a look at this would you eh"* I thought my leg was bad as I held back a gasp. His back was a mass of impressive colors and said, *"Looks great can't see anything wrong at all"* Andy said, *"Yeah Right eh you asshole!"* We still liked to talk Canadian.

We learned to say EH a lot after going to Canada and thought it was cool. Andy looked at the dogs outside the tent and calmly said nice doggies. Andy was a cool character. Bill explained that his family bred Rottweilers, big powerful dogs, and trained them to be attack dogs. They had owned a convenience store back in the suburbs of Chicago and got

robbed a couple of times, which prompted them to get a couple of these dogs. "*We liked them so much we started to breed them.*" They never got robbed again, but my thought was, "*I wonder how their business was with these dogs hanging around, because no way I'm getting out of this tent until these dogs are put away.*" So, I said, "Put the F******* dogs away I got to pee like a race horse."

Being some what sober now, we had a chance to look around at our surroundings. We were at a nice flat clearing in the middle of the woods with only a little dirt track leading in through dense woods. With the trailer on the car, our first thought was how the heck are we going to get out. Billy suggested that we take the trailer off and move it, turn the car around and put it back on or leave it here. He said, "*The boat's not floatable, is it? You won't need to be hauling it around. Just leave it here.*" He then showed us the beautiful small lake that was not far away but couldn't be seen from our campsite. Billy put the dogs in his truck and then helped us manhandle the trailer, so we could follow him to town. No way were we getting into his truck with those dogs.

After we grabbed some breakfast at the town café, we went to his tavern. His family was cleaning the bar and kitchen. They served lunch and dinner and seemed to be a bit overwhelmed. Through the years of living in the Northwoods it is amazing how many people have the dream of moving to the Northwoods and opening a bar or restaurant not realizing what that may entail. I believe this is the cause of these businesses to fail. Billy's family fit into this category. They lived their whole life in a suburb of Chicago and never owned a restaurant. And I believe they had no clue of the amount of work that went into it. It looked like that may be the case here, and little did we know then, what was to come in the future.

We spent the day hanging with Billy's friends. We went to a swimming quarry complete with swinging rope and ended back in the tavern for a night of shooting pool, chasing women and partying hard. We ended up taking the party back to the campsite and one of Billy's friends, a local Indian from a reservation close by, ended up staying the night. There seemed to be some tension and we did not feel all that comfortable being thrown into hanging with Bill's crowd. In retrospect, since my wife Marcia and I have lived in two small towns, one of 150 people where everyone was related and after twelve years of living there everyone thought we were related also. The second, is the Northwoods town, where we live today, which has about 1000 people but only about 200 full time residents.

This has given us more insight now about why we felt uncomfortable. Small towns have their own unique dynamic, which unless you have experienced it, it may be hard to understand, but here goes. They are usually divided into groups, first locals and non-locals, and then by relatives and non-relatives and if it is a tourist town, tourist and non-tourist, and so on. Well, you get the idea. In Wisconsin, the bars and churches are the center of the social net work, with alcohol being a big part also. It is like being thrown back in a high school social scene. It was not until we moved up to Wisconsin and after we had already had our campground and canoe livery for almost ten years that we found out what a FIB was. It stands for F###### Illinois Bastard. Billy, his family, Andy and I were all from Illinois. Well, duh we were all FIBS in Mellen and probably the locals really hated our guts. After a few days of this routine, we talked Billy into coming with us to paddle the Flambeau River for a couple of days. I said, *"Hey Billy want to go and check the Flambeau River with us for a couple of days?"* "I don't know. I have a baseball game tomorrow," he replied. I said, "*We still have a lot of time. We could leave the day after your game.*" Billy replied, "*I have an aluminum canoe that we could use since yours has a hole in it and leaks like a sieve!*" I replied, "*Well alrighty! We have some left-over food from our trip. All we need is a good bottle of whiskey.*"

LOTS OF NAKED GIRLS ON A ROCK

We knew, not being completely stupid, and having a canoe guide book that the North Fork of the Flambeau had class II rapids on it. Now, I realize, after a lifetime of paddling, how subjective ratings rapids are, but at least after wrecking one canoe, we decided to be smart and put to good use the tube that tried to kill us. The idea of putting floatation in a canoe is to displace water, stabilize the boat by having less water movement in the boat, helping the canoe float high in a capsize, and hopefully not pin against anything like a tree or a rock. In addition, the tube in the center of the boat would provide a comfortable seat for the third rider. We did not know then how important that this was going to be!

We dropped off Billy's car, which we took for the shuttle, remembering how far we had to walk for the Bois Brule shuttle, and because we had no back seat in Andy's car, at the end of our planned trip. Then we continued on, with Billy crammed in the back to the start of our trip, which was the beginning of river just below the Turtle-Flambeau flowage. We did not get an early start because the drive was about an hour and half so it was after lunch before we started to paddle. We are now getting smarter and did not bring a big cooler of beer, only a bottle of whisky, but weren't too smart cause we may again not have brought enough food. You'll learn a little more on that, a little later.

It was not long before we hit the first rapid, which had big waves but had relatively easy chutes and had no problems. Soon we could hear the second rapid, rounded a corner and low and behold, every guy's wet dream, there is a bunch of girls sunning naked on some rocks about ten feet above river. I MEAN NAKED! We almost didn't make the next rapid because were so shook up and excited. Don't you know we just had to stop with the testosterone running freely. We landed just below the rapid, luckily found a good spot, and camped. We began walking in search of the girl's camp. And remember we were young and are hormones were going wild, to get the skinny. HA!

We found their camp, traversing across some rough country, and quickly found out by talking to the counselor that this was a Girl Scout group and the girls were fifteen, or in other words, jail bait. We felt a little foolish and disappointed, or most of us did, but we behaved and went back to camp and our bottle of Whiskey. We had a good meal and were sitting around the fire, enjoying some good whiskey, when Billy informed us of his plan to go visit the girls. He said, "I *overheard some of them talking about sleeping on the ledge, where we saw them sun bathing."* Andy said, *"Are you sure this is a good idea"*? Billy replied, *"Why not?"* I came back with, *"Their jail bait."* He said, *"So, who would know?"* Andy and I did not want any part of this. We were 24 and yes young and full of cum, but really, we were nice and knew this was a real bad plan. We then began to emphatically try to discourage Billy from this fool's mission.

Billy had been stuck in the Town of Mellen, which did not have much in way of women to choose from, and was obviously a horn dog. We tried to stop him from going by arguing the morality of invading a Girl Scout camp and it was pitch dark out to boot. No way, Billy was hell bent to go, propped up by a few drinks this must have made sense to him. He took a little pen light and off he went.

It seemed like forever, and about a half of bottle of whiskey latter, when Billy returned. All the time he was gone we were wondering what in heck had happened. *"Did he get shot? -* "*no would have heard that.*" "*Did he get stabbed or did they tie him up and were torturing him?* "*We could understand that"* we pondered, *"Did he get lost?* "*Maybe"* "*Did he score"* "*We really hoped not."* Finally, with down cast eyes, he wandered in, went and got the inner tube and sat down by the fire. He did not say a word, but was obviously in much discomfort and bummed out. Andy inquired," *Hey Bill what the heck happened eh?"* No answer! We passed him the whiskey bottle and waited. After several drinks, he finally told his story.

He said," I *made my way toward where I thought the camp was and forgot that there was this crevasse where the girls were camped and proceeded to fall in, whacked my tail bone really bad, and got stuck. I couldn't figure out how to get out and was worried I would have to spend the night there and hoped you would have eventually come looking for me. Finally, with one last desperate try, I made it and hobbled back to camp."* All the time he was relating the story Andy and I were trying hard not laugh our heads off. Well, after a while, we just couldn't contain ourselves, and laughed like hyenas enjoying a fresh kill and shouted *"Whore Dog"* and a new knick name was born.

We continued on the next morning, not as early as we would have liked, because of the late night and Billy was moving slow. The early camp the day before put us behind schedule so we knew we were in for a long day. To make matters worse in started to rain. Karma was getting back at us, and we let the "Whore Dog" know who was to blame. It was a good thing that we had our floatation tube because if we didn't Billy would be in deep shit, with a probably broken tale bone. We had many rapids to go through, but our crude technique of switching sides all the time and obvious chutes got us through. We were shy on food again so we started to fish and Andy hooked into a large Red Dog Carp. Carp do not have the best repetition as a culinary delight, but we were hungry. We attempted to make a fire with no luck because it is raining. So, we cleaned the fish and tried that Sushi thing! Let me tell you if Carp isn't good cooked it really isn't good raw. Needless to say; it was a bad idea. We had trouble finding a camp that night but found one late, ate the rest of our food, which was not much, and went to bed hungry.

The next day we got up, had the last of our oatmeal and off we went chanting Cheeseburgers! *Cheeseburgers!* A little de ja vous there. We really didn't have all that far to go. We did our shuttle and were off to find Cheeseburgers, and back to Mellen.

We learned a couple more things on this trip. First, don't be lured by a bunch of naked girls. Well, you can't blame us too much for that! They could have been legal. Second-real bad idea to go looking for Girl Scouts in the dark that are jailbait! Third-Still have to work on that food thing! Fourth-Raw Carp tastes terrible! Fifth, inner tubes make great seats if you have a broken tailbone. And last, but not the least, if you want to have great memories you have to have excellent adventures.

QUEST

Back in Mellen, we continued with the party thing and were having a great time teasing Billy, who was still a hurting puppy. And all was great. We were well into the second day of partying when Andy in a drunken haze at 12am had a brilliant idea. He said, *"Hey let's go find my brother and cousin and take them kayaking on the Brule."* I replied, *"Let's go!"* Well, you may not think this was such a brilliant idea, but when one has been partying for a couple of days with some crazy locals you may understand. Andy's brother was vacationing with some of their cousins and families at Spooner Wisconsin. We looked on our map and it didn't seem that far away, maybe sixty or seventy miles. We had no idea where they were staying, but in our buzzed state, we figured how many resorts could there be in Spooner? We had whiskey, the car was full, and off we went on a Quest. We had a good half hour machine going, arriving in Spooner around 2:00am, and checked every resort we stumbled onto. There is a hell of a lot more resorts in Spooner than we figured! I'm sure you are not surprised that we were not going to be defeated and just kept checking resorts. We knew that Andy's younger brother Mike, who was eighteen at the time, and their cousin Vic, who was also eighteen, had borrowed Vic's older sister's nice newer model Dodge, for the trip, which Andy would recognize. We were getting a little discouraged but we were having fun and, on a quest, so we just kept checking resorts and at about 3:30 we found them. I think we were both surprised, because REALLY! We found them. We knocked on the door or should I say pounded, with Andy yelling, *"Get up you bums!"* So of course, we woke them up from a deep sleep, which they didn't appreciate with Andy's brother coming to door screaming, *"Who the F*** is out there?"* Andy replied, *"Get up you bums it's time to have some fun."* Mike said, *"Pat is that you?"* Andy's family called him Pat, Andy's middle name, because Andy's dad also was an Andy. Andy said, *"Of course it's me. Who do you think it is?"* Mike opened the door with his mouth open not knowing what to say. We began selling them on what an excellent adventure it would be to go kayak the Bois Brule. Nobody including us had ever been in a kayak, although we left that out. We also left the part out about how it had kicked our ass already, just a week and a half ago. There was a five-year difference between Andy and his brother and we used this to our advantage to convince them, maybe bully would be more accurate, to throw their lot in with us. They quickly packed their car and off we went. Our plan, because Andy and I were beat by now, was to catch a couple of Zs at the state campground by the Bois Brule that we had stayed at before. We got there at about dawn, set the tent up and crashed for about 4 hours.

We broke camp, had a quick breakfast of granola bars, and off to the canoe and kayak livery we went. The first thing the outfitter said to us, which I can appreciate now being in the same business was, *"do you boys have any experience in running whitewater?"* Andy and I being hotshots, "don't you know", we informed him that we were experts and had just paddled the river in our canoe. *Yeah Right*! I thought but managed to keep a straight face. He then asked us what section we wanted to paddle. Of course, it had to be the section that kicked our ass and wrecked my canoe. We left that part out of our expert resume. We got our kayaks and a ride to the put in and our excellent adventure was about to begin.

Luckily, the outfitter left before we attempted to get in our little whitewater kayaks, because it was not pretty and our expert status would have been in great jeopardy. Mike said, *"How do we get into these boats?"* I said being a hotshot. *"I'll show you"* and promptly tipped over. Now, after teaching whitewater for the last 30 years, I know that whitewater kayaks have rounded sides which makes them easy to roll back up after a capsize, but being idiots, also makes it very easy to turn over, which we all did with out further adieu. This was a tad discouraging but Vic, the athletic type, quickly caught on. Being the macho dudes that we thought we were, we couldn't be out done by Vic. We quickly found out, if you keep paddling hard, the boats were more stable, and when sitting still you were at most risk of turning over, which always happened when you least expected it. Mike was having a blast pretending he was drowning when his kayak turned over with him underneath trying to keep his head underwater. Or I should say we were having a blast laughing like hyenas watching this. "Uh Oh," we thought, *"Maybe he wasn't pretending."*

We all wondered what the upcoming whitewater was going to be like. And we could barely stay upright and the boats turned over so easy, because they were short, and wouldn't go in a straight line. It was not long before we hit our first rapid. At this point at least half of us were wondering, what the heck we had gotten ourselves into. Andy and I had the increased knowledge that the last two rapids were, the ledges, which put a hole in our canoe, and the Mays, which almost killed us, and we were understandably apprehensive. He said to me when we were out of hearing range from Vic and Mike. *"Should we tell them about the rapids coming up?"* I said, *"What good would it do? It will only make them scared."* Andy said, *"I'm scared now."* I said, *"No shit Sherlock!"* They almost killed us *before, but we have to act cool."* Andy said, *"Yeah Right!* We kept this to ourselves and everyone, maybe not Mike, was in a festive mood.

To our great dismay and delight the kayaks did great in the whitewater. They were more stable and steered easy. We were all now having way too much fun, and realized that the boat design was purposely made to tip you over when standing still so you wouldn't freak out if you flipped in whitewater, which we did, but not too much. Some of us, (Vic) didn't flip at all!

We finally neared the end of our trip and had made good time because you had to keep paddling if you didn't want to flip, and we were approaching the ledges. Andy and I, because we had intimate knowledge of the ledges, walking through them in our canoe, did not tell them that, took the lead and we had no problems. *"On to the Mays"* we all shouted, *"We can handle this sucker!"* We had that hotshot mojo thing going and just blasted right through without a hitch. *"There's our landing, Yeah,"* we shouted! Uh Oh! How do get out of these kayaks? The only way we knew, and had a lot of experience at, was to just tip them over!! Vic of course was a show off and rammed his boat on shore and climbed out. Who to figure.

We learned a few good lessons on this excellent adventure. First, never underestimate the power of a quest. Second, if you are the older brother, you can bully your younger brother. I already knew this being a younger brother. Third, the right equipment makes all the difference. Fourth, maybe when someone looks like they are drowning they may need help. Mike, with great loudness, taught us this lesson. Last, but not the least, if you want to have great memories you have to have excellent adventures.

BANG!

We changed into dry clothes and headed for Mellen. Mike and Vic were following us, when suddenly they started to flash their lights and pulled over. We pulled over to see what the problem was. Vic said, "*We heard a big bang.*" We said, "*Yeah Right!*" We all looked the car over and did not see anything wrong, and off we went to get those cheeseburgers and beer at Billy's place. We got there and still did not realize that there was anything wrong, went into the restaurant, ordered cheeseburgers and beer and proceeded to introduce our younger friends to the crazy world of Mellen and Billy's friends. Mike and Vic were ecstatic to be able to drink and party with us being the young age of nineteen.

After partying for a couple of hours we all decided, not surprisingly after the last couple of days to head to our now, very familiar camp site on Billy's property. They were following us in on the dirt tract road, and came to the campsite and parked. When they got out of their car, they said, "*We think we smell gas.*" It was dark now so we got our flashlights and started looking under the car and to our shock, we found a steady stream of gas coming from the bottom of the gas tank.

"*Uh Oh! Not good!*" I said, "*Let's try and plug the hole with a screw.*" We then proceeded to try to plug the hole, which of course made things worse with a bigger stream of gas coming out. No duck tape, nothing. "*OK*" we thought, being wise to the explosive nature of gas fumes, we decided that the best thing to do was to set camp up and let the gas drain and then push the car away by hand from the gas and fumes.

I was arranging things inside our tent when I heard a large bang! In a blast of adrenalin I blasted, no pun intended, out of the tent to see, with great shock, the car was completely engulfed in flames. Everyone now was thunderstruck by this sight. It was just like in the movies with flames shooting thirty feet into the air. "*NOT GOOD!*" we all thought. I shouted to Vic and Mike "*Get the cooler and go to lake and get water.*" "*Where's the lake?*" they replied in a panic. I pointed to where it was; you could not see it easily from the campsite and said, "*Over there down the hill. Hurry the whole forest may go up!*" They grabbed the cooler and raced down the hill. We were trapped in the middle of the forest in August by a burning car with trees surrounding it. Really not good!! We sprang into action and Andy and I started trying to put out the fire around the car. We were using sticks and our feet when. Bang!! Another big explosion. To my horror, Andy got knocked right to the ground. I cried, "*Are you all right?*" He soon got up and said, "*I think so*" and fought on. We had several more explosions when different things blew up, like the gas can, outboard motor, insect spray and who knows what all, and fought on with Vic and Mike throwing water around the car and Andy and I trying to control the spread of the fire. We all thought that we were going to die and discussed retreating into the lake or trying to figure which way to run if the forest caught fire. Meanwhile, we continued frantically fighting the fire and all of us thought help had to be coming soon, because we knew there was a fire tower that was not far away. And by God we had a huge fire burning. Somebody just had to see it. *NOT!* We kept fighting and the car kept burning and burning and burning. It had now died down some and was only about a ten-foot blaze. And we began to relax a little. *"Looks like we just might escape death again,"* I thought. Finally, Andy said, *"I think we are safe now; it doesn't look like the*

fire will spread." I said, *"Let's get the hot dogs."* They looked at me like I was crazy. I said, *"Nothing wrong with a little levity."* We should be thankful that we are all alive and nobody got hurt." We did not know it then, that Andy was blown into a poison ivy patch, which became apparent in the next couple of days. *Vic said, "Yeah right! Look at my sister's car. What am I going to tell her?"* Andy said, *"You're alive. It's just a car."* Mike said, *"We lost all of our clothes and my uncle's motor and how are we going to get home?"* Andy said, *"You can ride in the canoe on the trailer there's plenty of room and we have raincoats if it rains."* He was into the levity thing also, trying to cheer up the boys, although it wasn't working too well.

It's amazing how long a car will burn. And we were all now hungry and wished we did have some hot dogs to cook and opened a few beers that we had left. We were all dead tired after our epic battle and what we went through the last couple of days, so we went to bed.

When we got up the next morning we were amazed at how long and how much of a car will burn. And wondered how the heck the forest did not catch fire, and why didn't anybody come. I think it was a maple tree that was closest; it was hard to tell what it was, because all the leaves and area around the car was charred. The car was sitting on its rims. The tires burned the longest. And just a metal ring was left of the steering wheel. All the seats and dash were gone except for a frame and a few springs. All the glass had melted along with some of the metal. The only thing that could identify what kind of car it was is a partially melted emblem, which we thought Vic could hand to his sister when she asked where her car was. Andy said, *"Hey Vic, here is the car emblem you can give to your sister."* Vic and Mike had a gray green sheen about them and I thought they may pass out. They just stared blankly back at us not saying a word. We knew that someday this would be a great story and memory but not so much now.

As the trauma was fading, we began to wonder how the car had caught on fire. Mike and Vic were young, had not ever experienced anything even close to this kind trauma, and of course were a little bummed out, no that's not right, they were a lot bummed out. Well, if I think about it, not many people have experienced this kind of trauma. You might be able to relate to how they felt after losing all their clothes, fishing gear, out board motor, and of course, sister's pretty new car. We consoled them with the standard; at least nobody got hurt etcetera, rhetoric and tried to make light of everything, but nothing helped.

Vic was the closest to the car when it blew, so of course was the one we figured had something to do with it. He never fessed up, but we speculated that he had the lantern in his hand, which he said he did. And went to get something out of the trunk and put the lantern down, where the gas fumes would congregate, and bang. Everyone should be aware of how volatile gas fumes are.

Even when you fill your car up, your cell phone or static electricity can ignite the fumes. So, doesn't it make sense if you put down a Colman lantern or even get it close to the car with all that gas on the ground and the fumes, that it would go ka boom, which it did. Duh! I guessed he spaced out, and we really can't blame him after the last couple of days we had.

We then decided we needed to go to town to call the insurance company and get something to eat. Uh! Oh! That's when we realized that we were trapped and could not get Andy's car around the burned-out car. This is when the tree removal began. We figured if we took a couple of these little trees out, we could squeeze the car out. The trouble was, we only had a dull ax. Finally, with manly brute force and an hour-long struggle, we got the trees out and the car was free. We went to town, called the insurance company and police, who both turned out to be great, and met them back at the car with a flat bed truck. Both of them could not believe that nobody, especially with the close fire tower, saw the fire, and wondered, as we did, how the heck the forest did not catch fire. We all thought that some heads were going to roll over this.

We then went to Billy's and informed them of all that had taken place and they were good and grateful that nobody got hurt. It turned out that it was not the last fire that would affect their lives greatly. The next year, one night, after I am sure a night of partying, Billy and his Indian friend crashed upstairs and lost their lives in a fire. Billy's friend was on the couch and Billy was in his bedroom. They speculated that his friend went to sleep with a cigarette, which caught the couch on fire. Billy was found in the hall going to help his friend who was found by the couch, both succumbed to fumes and the whole place burned to the ground. Billy, a great loss, was twenty-five years old. You may be wondering where Billy's parents were. Well, as with many a dreaming city folk, they shut the business down, and went back to the city.

We rigged some stuff to make a place for the boys to sit in the back seat. They were relieved that they didn't have to ride in the canoe. Remember, we had taken the seat out and borrowed some clothes for Mike and Vic and hit the road. We had a great half hour machine going consoling Mike and Vic and trying to figure out a way to tell his sister when we got back. We finally decided that simply giving her the melted emblem told it all.

When we arrived home Vic's sister took the lost of her car well, and was most grateful that nobody got hurt. Vic and Mike I think finally got over it and Andy and I moved on to more excellent adventures.

We learned a lot from this experience. First, never ignore a big bang. Second, gas fumes are very volatile and extreme precautions must be taken. Third, always have an escape route. Fourth, never be without hotdogs. You never know when a roasting fire might pop up. Last, but not the least, if you want to have great memories you have to have excellent adventures.

GMC

To make a living supporting these excellent adventures you should recall that I am a professional musician and to supplement this, I taught piano. During this time, I drove around a lot to different student's houses and came upon a nice-looking GMC pickup truck for sale on the side of the road. I took the number down on the For Sale sign and gave the guy a call. He said it was a one-ton truck that was used in his cement business, very reliable, extremely heavy duty, and only had about 50,000 miles on it. I arranged to meet him, liked the truck and price and became the proud owner of a real heavy-duty four speed manual transmission, large straight six-cylinder pick-up truck. The first gear was so low you could push a tree over with it. I had a friend who was selling a camper cap for a truck and went to check it out. It had a bed over the cab, heater, ice box, stove and cabinets on the side. All that was needed to make this an excellent adventure machine was to finish the truck bed with walls, bins over the wheel wells and a floor.

It didn't take long for Andy, Gary B, a friend, and I to hatch a plan for a maiden voyage of the excellent adventure truck. We all got together and in a few days of feverous work, got the job done. I acquired a nice van bench seat when I bought the cap, which we placed just below the overhang of the upper bed. This served as a step up to the bed, an extra bed, and an excellent party seat. We also made seats on top of the boxes we made for the wheel wells. Now, here is the real cool thing, especially if you are party animals as we were then. It was legal to consume alcohol while on the road, because there was no connection between front and back. Well to be honest that may have been one of the reasons I bought the heavy-duty truck and cap. The other reason was to haul my keyboards and band playing stuff around.

It was February in Chicago and we thought the Florida Keys, which none of us had ever been to, sounded like a good idea, plus we could check out Mardi Gras in New Orleans on the way to the Keys. We thought this was a perfect maiden voyage for the GMC. We thought it would be a great idea if we could find a fourth person, then we could have two up front and two in the back. The two people up front could each drive 4 hours and the people in back could party and sleep for eight. This way we could go non-stop, be legal and safe up front, and do what ever in the back. Andy then had a brilliant idea, *"Hey, a girl Robin from work whose boyfriend had just dumped her, was depressed and might be interested in a road trip. She said she had a friend down in Florida that she wanted to visit around Orlando and Disney World. I'll ask her if she wants to go."*

Andy asked Robin and she was way up for it. We had our fourth and now on to our supplies. With such a big heavy-duty truck, which holds a lot. And we may have over done it a bit on the alcohol. We brought four cases of beer, and a half gallon each of whiskey, gin and vodka. We also had lots of food, snacks and mix, along with all of our other stuff, which fit with no problem. We even had room to spare, in the GMC. We left the next morning and drove to Chicago to pick up Robin. Being three young optimistic and unattached males who were going to be traveling a long way with an unattached female on the rebound we devised a plan to prevent any jealousy problems that may accrue. Being very practical, we decided that we would take turns partnering with Robin. One day each sounded like a reasonable plan. Of course, we never mentioned this to Robin when we picked her up. Robin was cute, well endowed, (yes, we are pigs) and had a very easy and reasonable personality. Perfect! Off we went on the first of many excellent adventures in the GMC.

I don't remember how we decided this, but Gary was to be first, Andy second, and I last on the totem pole, which turned out not to work so well for me, but I got over it. Andy and I had a great half hour machine going and eight hours later, we ended up in Carbondale where Andy, his brother, and cousins had all gone to school at Southern Illinois University. His one cousin Jimmy had bought a spread outside of Carbondale and we thought we would stop, visit and see his new place. It was impressive, complete with a great pond and lots of flowering Daffodils. Jimmy said, *"I don't know what I'm going to do with all these dam daffodils."* The light went off in my brain and I said, *"Let's go to campus and sell them. We could use the money for more beer."* He said, *"Great idea!"* We picked a crap load of flowers, bought a crap load of beer, and went to the campus to make some money. We found a nice spot to park the GMC, got out our cooler, flowers, chairs and proceeded to sell a crap load of flowers by shouting. *"Daffodils are a buck, sips are free"* and got a great buzz going to boot.

With our new found cash in our pockets and a fun day under our belts we said our goodbyes to Jimmy and continued on to New Orleans. Gary and I drove and Robin and Andy moved to the back. Gary said that he and Robin had gotten along just fine and had a great time. About eight hours later we arrived in New Orleans and Mardi Gras.

There were lots and lots of people. Being young and of course stupid and paranoid, I had a knife on me. It didn't take long before an undercover cop came up and said, *"Hey you got a knife on you?"* *"Holy crap, I'm going to jail,"* I thought. He was padding me down while he said this and I was twisting my body trying to keep him away from my back pocket where the knife was located. By some miracle the under-cover Cop managed somehow not to feel the knife. *"Thank God!"* I thought. With all the people and hassle, this was the last straw for me and Gary agreed. Andy and Robin had already gone back to the camper. When we got back to the camper, we thought better of bothering the happy couple in the back of the truck and blew out of town. Technically, there should have been a switch in partners at New Orleans, but how can you interrupt a happy couple having fun. The next driver cycle Andy switched with Robin who came up front with me and soon we were near Orlando and Disney World.

Disney World had only been open a short while so we all decided to go check it out for a day. If you have been to Disney World recently, you know how crowded it can be. It was a weekday, brand new and was not crowded at all. It didn't have all the worlds or rides it has today, but we managed to have a blast. I, so far, didn't have much time to get to know Robin yet, but we were hanging, having fun and the vibes were good. I truly believe that long before this Robin had figured out what our plan was and happily went along. Robin's friend lived not far from Disney world so we dropped her off and said our sad goodbyes because she was flying back to Chicago after her visit with her friend. We were now down to three. We were all sad to see Robin go, especially me. She was an excellent traveling companion and I think we all helped Robin work through her breakup with love and understanding. Man, that's a crock, what I meant to say is, we all helped Robin get through her breakup with a huge amount of partying and a real excellent adventure and hope her life has turned out well, which she greatly deserved.

We blasted down to the Keys and stopped in Key Largo to check out the under-water reserve park. We got our first experience snorkeling in the ocean. It was beautiful and not anything like the snorkeling that we had done in a quarry just across the street from where I lived. Did I mention that we had brought spear guns along? We tried but they did not allow spear guns in the park. Who would figure a reserve not allowing us to kill fish? That prompted us to move to peruse our murderous ways in the little coves off Key Largo in a quest to bag some big fish.

We found a perfect little cove right off RT 1. We got our gear and were quickly in the water loaded for bear, looking for fish. It was not long before we spied a huge barracuda. *"Uh! Oh! Not going to shoot at that!"* pondering if I was the one who was being hunted. We soon found a school of fish but man they can move fast, real fast. We tried to split up and hunt like a pack of hungry wolfs chasing fish to each other. We had a blast but we were stupid kids, so not surprisingly no luck, but loads of fun, and we were fortunate that we did not shoot each other.

We decided to move down the keys to Marathon key and stayed at a cool State Park that had campsites right on the beach. The next day we arranged a snorkeling trip with a small boat, and out to the reef again, we went. This part of the reef was not a protected park, so we could use our spears and get some dinner. We got into the water and the first thing we saw was is a large barracuda, maybe four feet long. *"UH OH not good again!"* There were schools of barracuda, with big teeth. The reason why we never got busted for anything is we did know when to chill. So, we just paddled along with our spear guns to see what would happen next. Not one us, at this point, had any thought of trying to spear one. Like

I said we were dumb sometimes but not stupid. The barracuda finally left the scene and now went back to the hunt. Incredibly, we finally got a nice big round fish. We hurried back to the boat, being mindful of the barracuda, where the captain informed us angrily that this was an angelfish, which was not good to eat, and usually admired and not shot. OOPS! We continued to hunt when Andy noticed this wallet floating in the water. I dove down to take a look and while underwater realized there was a lot of money in it. When I got to the surface, I signaled Gary, who was floating nearby, to show him our incredible luck. He comes over excitedly looking at the wallet and all the money, and suddenly realizes that it's his wallet. *"Oh my God!"* He exclaims, *"I forgot to take it out of my pocket."* He was snorkeling in cut offs. Gary was incredibly thankful and knew how lucky he was that he did not lose his wallet with all his money, license and everything. He exclaimed, *"Let's go to Key West! The drinks are on me."*

After arriving back at the dock, with a not too happy captain, we headed for Key West, the last Key, which is not far from Marathon Kay where we were camping. Back in the early seventies Key West had not yet metamorphosed into the commercial place that it is now, and still fit the image that Hemmingway had painted in his books. Of course, we had to hit every bar, and we did our party thing really well that night. We were young but we started at an early age and had lots of practice, and fit right in with the locals. Jimmy Buffet would have been proud of us.

The next morning, we had astronomical hangovers but nothing new about that. When we were around Disney World we had stocked up on some fresh oranges and grapefruit, that along with the clean ocean air quickly got us back on our feet. The brakes were not good on the truck and since we had hangovers already, we decided to spend the day doing a brake job at our campsite.

There is one advantage in being young with not a lot of money. If you want something fixed you had to do it yourself. All of us fit into, the not much money thing, and we all had experience in working on our cars. We also had brought a good set of tools, another plus having a lot of storage. Marathon Key, where we were staying, is one of the biggest keys and the shopping was good. It did not take us long to locate a parts store and what we needed. We had a policy of making work fun, so of course we were partaking in a few beers while working. The brake job went well and took most of the day. What didn't go well was that Andy got an incredible headache because we think the beer and hot sun dehydrated him, another one of those learning moments. He drank a bunch of water and took it easy and the next day he was fine

Our time for this trip was beginning to run short so we decided to begin to head north. We had to change our routine now, because there was only three. So, what we did was to have the rider switch to the driver, who then went to the back to become the sleeper or more often than not the mixer. This system worked pretty well but encouraged us all to be buzzed at once, which was not too wise. On our way back we thought we would stop and buy a bunch of oranges to take home. We were also out of liquor and thought how great a screwdriver would be with fresh oranges, and so we bought a bottle of 151 proof Smirnoff, again not wise. It was Andy's turn to be in back, which made him the mixer of drinks. He did this by cutting oranges in half and squeezing two at once in separate glasses. We got pretty buzzed really quickly. It was a good thing the GMC's top speed was about 60 and it liked to go about 55. We stopped at a rest area to take a leak and when I pulled out, I didn't notice at first, that Gary, who had switched to the mixing responsibilities was running behind the truck with a couple of drinks in his hands screaming for us to stop. Good thing I check my mirrors a lot.

When I look back at these times, I wonder how we never got thrown in jail. We certainly deserved it. On the other hand, we never crossed the line into complete insanity and had just enough paranoia, installed in all of us by our strict parents, to keep us out of jail and alive. Way to go parents.

We are getting smarter by the day, and learned some lessons from this trip. First, you can really make tracks in a camper with four drivers. Second, girls who get dumped by boyfriends make great traveling companions. Third, Mardi Gras wasn't as good as it is advertised. Fourth, leave the knife and your paranoia behind. Fifth, Disney World was much better back before it was so crowded. Sixth, always check pants pockets if you are going to swim in cutoffs. Seventh, always check your mirror for someone running behind your vehicle, that you are about to leave behind. Eighth, if you are drinking beer in the sun, drink a lot of water also. Last, but not the least, if you want to have great memories you have to have excellent adventures.

HOW TO WRECK A FRIEND'S CANOE

At this point, I still mistakenly believed, that I was a hot shot in a canoe. I met Mike E., who worked with my brother. He was a jazz guitarist and we became friends through jamming together. And played for several years in a couple of different bands. My brother, Mike and I all wanted to get away and take a road trip. Mike had a nice new Grumman canoe, and if you remember the state of our canoe (hole in it from Bois Brule); I suggested we take his and spend our time doing a couple of rivers in northern Wisconsin. I've always enjoyed planning trips and have done so, for most of my life. Being a self-professed hot shot, they took my advice and we were off to the Wolf River. The guidebook that I was using suggested that the section of the river we were planning to paddle was only appropriate for intermediate paddlers who have had experience in paddling Class II whitewater. Well, I thought, *"I had experience paddling class II rapids."* They were apprehensive, from this description. I said, *"No problem, I have done the Bois Brule, Flambeau, Mississagi, and Blah, blah, blah, we can handle it. I'll show you how to paddle."* Here's the choices thing again. I see many people in our canoe business that are just as I was at this time, a dumb self-professed hot shot, who had no business giving any advice. I talked a good game and they trusted me. Oh Boy, that turned out great! Not! We loaded the canoe on top of Mike's car and off we went. I was suffering from food poisoning, which made the 5-hour ride up to the Wolf River interesting to say the least.

The next day I was feeling better and we decided to do section two of the Wolf River, which has some class II whitewater. We put on our life jackets, loaded a small cooler and some snacks and off we went. Because we had three men in a tub and all wanted to paddle, I devised a bizarre technique where the two of them would switch sides at my command and I would rudder at the back to steer. Remember they trusted that I knew what I was doing! *Yeah right*! We had time to practice this technique on some small and easy rapids and had no problems and we were all feeling good about our skills. Then, Uh Oh! we could hear the next rapid from a good distance away. Mike said, *"Sounds like a good rapid ahead are you sure we can handle It?"* "Hell, we got no problems. We're experts," I exclaimed! We rounded the corner and saw what looked like some big waves and lots and lots of rocks, with no clear path to take. *"Oh No, where is the chute?"* I thought. I screamed at everyone that we had to paddle harder, not having a clue as to which way to go with Mike screaming, *'I don't see a good way to get through.'* The boat hit a big submerged rock and quickly turned sideways, toward the side that they were paddling on, and quickly filled with water. We were pinned. Luckily, we were able to jump out and only got partially wet.

A canoe, like our seventeen-foot Grumman, can hold around two hundred gallons of water. This is called displacement, which determines how much a canoe or any boat can float. The more water it displaces the more weight it can support and not sink. Water is heavy, weighing around eight pounds a gallon. If you do the math 200 x 8, it comes to 1600 pounds. That's a lot of weight!

If you go sideways into a rock the boat typically, especially if you are dumb like us, turns broad side and quickly fills up with water and is pinned against the rock. When you factor in the weight of the water and speed of the current, you can see that this is not a good scenario. These combined forces can quickly bend an aluminum canoe like a crushed beer can or rip a boat in half or at the very least, and can be very difficult to get it unpinned. This is exactly what happened to us. Luckily, the boat was not completely broad side so we were able to get it unpinned using all of our combined strength, and it did not suffer too much damage, but we were all soaked.

Being young and foolish, we did not quite understand the effects of cold wet clothes on the temperature of the body making your temperature drop. This is called hypothermia or the beginning of hypothermia. The first thing your body does when you get cold is your core temperature starts to drop and your body begins to pool your blood in your core in an attempt to keep your important organs warm. This unfortunately shorts your brain of blood making you spacey. We were not that cold yet, because we were only partially wet, but more to come.

We got the boat back upright and continued. My brother said, *"Hope that was the hardest rapid."* I said, *"It must be, I've done a lot of class II rapids but that's got to be a class III."* *"No shit Sherlock"* my brother replied. Soon we heard the tell-tale roar of a rapid again. I thought, *"Oh crap."* We rounded the corner and to my great dismay, this rapid looked even harder. Mike yelled, *"What do we do?"* I screamed back, *"Paddle hard, now switch, switch, switch"* and then bang, again we were sideways with water pouring into the boat, and us completely wet and now getting very cold. The Wolf River should have been called the "lots and lots of Rocks River.' In the rapids I was used to paddling there were clear paths, we call these chutes, which can be seen easily. These rapids had no clear paths so we crashed and pinned again. Each time the pinning was a little worse on the boat and we took more of a beating. The effects of being cold really affected our thinking as we all got spacey and did not seem to care. It was not long before we had our worse pin and could not get the boat out. We were now in real trouble! At this point, we were exhausted, light headed, freezing cold and did not know what to do. And then to our amazement and great relief, we see a canoe paddling upstream through the rapid that had kicked our ass so bad going in the right direction. They were always paddling on opposite sides, in perfect harmony with each other, using a lot of different strokes that I had no clue what they were. They were traveling quickly toward us in an obvious attempt to help, and boy did we need it! It did not take them long to get to us. They quickly got us unpinned and informed us the canoe resort where we left the car was right around the corner. I said, *"Thanks a lot, you really saved our butts. I don't know what I would have done if you had not shown up"* George said," *After we did the shuttle for you, we figured that you would have trouble and thought it would be wise if we came up the river and gave you a hand. I'm amazed you made it down this far."* I said, *"We pinned a bunch of times but managed to get ourselves out, but not this time. We are freezing cold and are really spacey."* George said, *"You are suffering from the effects of being cold and need to warm up quick. You should have no trouble from here and there is a warm shower waiting for you."* We all thanked George greatly and followed them back.

This was the first time I met George Steed, who is what I was destined to become in the future, but I didn't know that then. We made it to his resort with much relief. George said, *"You need to get out of those clothes right now, and hit the shower house."* My brother replied, *"Let's go, our dry clothes are in the car."* We were all shaking, like a bunch of convicts waiting to be hanged, but were soon in heaven as the water began to warm us up. We changed into dry clothes, and quickly set up our tent, the nice Eureka tent that Andy and I had brought, and made a large fire, with wood we brought from George, and had a great meal at George's restaurant.

I was humiliated with the knowledge that I was not a hotshot but just a dumb ass. I realize now, this was the necessary first step in becoming a hotshot. I have been a teacher my whole life and know how important it is to know when you are dumb. And to respect and learn from people who are smarter than you are.

George had a place back then that was similar to the place that we now have in Northern Wisconsin. He had a nice campground, canoe shop, livery and restaurant. The only thing we don't have is a restaurant. We had a great night of camping that night sitting around the fire with plenty to talk about. The canoe had taken a real beating. It had several major dents and bends. George and his helper helped us kick bang and jump on the canoe to get it back to resembling a canoe. I had noticed that the canoe George was paddling was not made out of aluminum. I said, *"Hey George what the heck are your canoes made out of. They look like they are in good shape, even with the beating they must take on your river from hell."* He said, *"They are very tough and designed to run whitewater."* Good naturally he continued. *"This is not a river from hell. You are just dumb asses."* The material he said was Royalex, which had just come on the market a few years before, and had revolutionized whitewater canoeing. I knew I had to get one of these boats and needed to learn how to paddle like George and his partner.

Sitting around the campfire dry, warm and with a full belly the world was looking up again. Mike, who was apprehensive about taking his never dinged new canoe on this trip in the first place and to his credit, had quickly gotten over his boat taking a real beating. Now that his boat was broken in, we discussed what to do for the rest of the trip. Having paddled the first section of the Flambeau with Billy and Andy. I suggested paddling a few days on the next sections of the river. Understandably, my creditability had taken a dive, so they talked to George who agreed and said that would be a much better place for us to paddle. What he really meant; it would be a much better place for you dumb-asses to paddle.

We got up the next morning to a beautiful warm sunny day we needed for the Flambeau. We had a lot to talk about from the adventures of the previous day making a great half hour machine and soon we were at an outfitter's place on the Flambeau. He gave us good suggestions and we planned to paddle from Nine Mile Creek down to his place on Highway W. This was an easy two-day trip. He said there were only easy rapids. We said, "*That sounds great. Are you sure this is a river for us dumb asses?*" He said, "*Just about all our customers are dumb asses, you will do fine.*"

When I saw George paddle, I noticed a few things and tried to mimic what I could remember. I noticed that he employed a stroke where he would reach to the side and draw the canoe sideways, while his partner would push the canoe from the opposite side. I thought this was cool because on the Wolf, when we tried to turn around a rock, we would be pushed right into it, because we were sideways to the current. We worked on this technique and it worked well. I also noticed, when were following George that they would back paddle a lot to slow the boat down. I thought this was a great idea, because when we went fast, we had no time to try to avoid rocks.

The outfitter's advice was good and we had no problems. The Flambeau is a lot bigger river with easily read chutes, which was better suited to our lack of paddling skills and began to realize why I thought I was a hotshot, when I was only a dumb ass. It is a very subjective thing to rate a rapid. And you have to realize that river levels change, making it harder or easier, and the level of paddling skills that the reviewer may have and what type of boat he had when making the review. So, my advice is to always scout a rapid, especially when on a canoe trip. And if you have any fears at all, portage, or line. On this part of the river, we enjoyed the very nice developed canoe campsites, complete with latrines and picnic tables. On the first section of the river that Andy, Billy and I had paddled, there were no developed campsites. Sometimes life was just too good. It's amazing how in a lot of our adventure's things may start out a little rough but always seem to turn out great. We finished the trip with no trouble and made our way home with a banged-up canoe, more knowledge, and our pride hurt, but still, fun was had by all.

You may have figured out by now that this is a story of how not to do things, which in turn shows you how to do things, because this is how I learned to become what I am today. We learn by having fun and by being dumb. I'm great at both those things. Here is what we learned from this trip. First, be leery of someone who claims to be an expert, but be receptive to the advice of a real expert. Second, don't trust guidebooks! Running rapids is very subjective. What is easy for a trained paddler may be very hard for a novice and so on. Third, wear clothes that do not absorb water, are warm and dry fast. It's a drag to be cold. Fourth, have some extra clothes in a dry bag if you get wet to warm you up, which also helps you make good decisions. You are better off being completely naked than having wet clothes on. Fifth, you may not be as smart as you think. Sixth, it is ok to be a dumb ass as long as you learn from it. Last, but not the least, if you want to have great memories you have to have excellent adventures.

THE TIMES THEY ARE A CHANGING

You may be wondering how I was able to have so many excellent adventures in my life, making it possible to pursue my dreams. I 'm going to talk a little bit about what was happening at these times in my other world, which lead to my concurring career as a canoe guide and instructor and lots of excellent adventures. I'm also going to talk about how I managed financially to pull this off. I have never made much money in my life and have followed one rule that I learned from my dad. Always live cheaper than the money you make. He always did this and invested his saved money in houses where we lived. He can thank my mother for this, because as I said earlier, she would get an itch to move about every seven or eight years. Her itches corresponded with, what I now know are the up and down cycles of real estate. I think most people do accept the wisdom of following this principle but with the event of easy credit, and an indulged generation, they may not know what this really means, and how to do it. Part of telling this story is how I accomplished this.

Shortly, after the band started, I moved in with another high school buddy, Chris, and his wife. Chris would be a part of a lot of the excellent adventures that I would have in the future. At this point, I was in school part time, teaching piano full time, and playing in a band. The summer time was slow for the band, teaching, and school, which made a lot of time for paddling and excellent adventures. These were great times, because none of us made a lot of money, and we made do by sharing living expenses and doing a lot together, also sharing the costs. We would have big parties and everyone would pitch in for the liquor and food. We rented the bottom half of a big house that was on the Fox River in Illinois and had a nice swimming quarry across the street. What a place to live! We lived just above a damn on the river and could canoe a long way up river before you hit any current. We had my canoe, which was repaired and now floated, stored behind our house, and spent a lot time canoeing on the river. We also had an empty lot that was owned by the same people we were renting from where we put up a volleyball net. OK, we had a river, big yard, volley ball court, and wonderful swimming quarry across the street. What does this all equate to, parties, lots of parties and fun.

Slowly, over the next couple of years the band took over the whole house and even the house next door, and Chris and his wife moved out during that time and got a nice little house on a farm that was dirt cheap to rent. It was not the Hilton, but they lived by the same rule for financial success. Eventually, things were not going well in the band and I decided it was time to move on. Chris said I could move in with them again and if I wanted, I could fix up part of an out building, that we had been using to work on vehicles, as a little apartment. The rent would be almost nothing and it sounded like a good plan. Chris and his wife were very mellow and easy to live with. I remember one time we were rebuilding the engine of the trash mobile in their living room. Chris's wife tolerated that for a while, but we had to work fast, and clean up exceptionally well.

As you know already, I had helped my dad do small projects and we had built our canoe, which was now mine, from a kit. But I never attempted anything like this. The building was really just a shell with no floor or anything else. Gary B. offered to help. He was an out of work carpenter and had the time. Because Gary was good, it was amazing that it only took about a couple of weeks to complete the project and I learned a lot. Keep in

mind we were not building deluxe accommodations. We made a floor, insulated and covered the walls, put a couple of lofts in, made some windows, and installed a space heater. There was no running water and no toilet. I could use the toilet in the house, and had a port a potty in the back of the GMC that I used at night and there was a hydrant out side where I could get water.

My place was no Ritz Carleton, but living almost on my own was a real treat, and I was able to save a lot of money. It was really like deluxe camping and trained me for what was to come later in my life. The worst part of living there was the other residence who resided in my little shack. There were massive amounts of mice and wolf spiders, and they were not about to give it up easily to me. A wolf spider is a large ugly and hairy spider with an average circumference of the size of a fifty-cent piece and get can get as large as a silver dollar. There was a continual battle being waged between me the spiders and the mice. The worse part was sleeping in the loft at night feeling the spiders and or mice run across my face. Not surprisingly, I did not succeed in getting too many women to stay over, although, a few of the good ones did manage to brave the elements.

I made it through the first winter and had acclimated to this life style when the proverbial roof fell in. Chris never told me that he didn't get permission from the owner of the farm. A farmer rented the farmland where the extra house and building were and told the owner about the extra tenant and my ass was kicked out. I moved to a trailer park and campground in the GMC about three miles away. This was my situation just before the next great adventure was about to begin.

BILL M.

Bill M., one of my three college buddies that, I have talked about earlier in this book, and hung around with, was now reduced to two, with Billy being killed in the fire, called me one day. He asked me if I wanted to go on an organized canoe trip with him, being guided by Tuck Well. He went on a backpacking trip with him the year before and said it was great, and liked him. I asked Bill how much and thought it might be nice to let someone else do all the planning and worrying for a change. Bill said, *"It was a two-week trip in North Eastern Canada on the Missinaibi River."* I did not know anything about this river, but it sounded exciting and was something I could afford. Bill and I paddled before on some local rivers and had taken a three-day trip on the South Fork of the Flambeau in Northern Wisconsin the year before. The Flambeau River trip went fine and we paddled well together, and even developed an interesting technique of paddling in low water on a river. Well, not really paddling, but kind of skate boarding with a canoe. We would each be on opposite sides of the canoe with one foot in and one foot out propelling us along. It worked pretty well, and little did I know then, how much we would use this technique later.

Bill told me that there was an orientation weekend coming up for people to get to know each other. And I needed to get the deposit in soon to get on the trip. I was skeptical, but since Bill had gone with this guide before I thought it may be a fun trip, and sent in my deposit.

The meeting place for the orientation weekend was at the Clock Tower Inn, a resort hotel just off the expressway in Rockford Illinois, at 6:00 pm on a Saturday. Bill called the day before and said something had come up and he could not be there. That should have been a warning sign, but this dumb ass did not take the hint. It was only about a half hour away and I thought in for a penny, in for a pound and decided to go. I had passed this resort many times before when heading to Wisconsin and had no problems finding it, in the dependable trash mobile. When I got there, I soon located our group. There were many folks from Chicago and the suburbs who had traveled a good distance to get there.

There was also a couple from Rockford. We were instructed to bring a sleeping bag and some snacks, and all were excited about the trip. Six o'clock came and no Tuck Well, our guide. Seven o'clock came and no Tuck Well. Along with Bill, some of the people on the trip had also gone with Tuck on a trip and assured the rest of us not to worry. Well Tuck, his girlfriend Jan, and another helper guide Mike showed up at about 7:45. Not a great start for the weekend and an ominous sign for the future.

TUCK WELL

Tuck introduced himself and apologized about being late. That was a good sign. He had said they had a hard time getting a projector to show us slides of some of his trips. That was a bad sign. We then piled into Tuck's big van and proceeded to a forest preserve somewhere in Rockford. By the time we arrived it was almost dark. He set up the projector and screen in a pavilion and showed us some slides of his trips, which did look cool, so I thought things were looking up, but wondered where we were going to spend the night? I also thought, there were no slides of any canoe trips, only back packing trips! That was another bad sign.

After the slide show, he talked about what everyone needed to bring on the trip. Having been on a lot of canoe trips, and to his credit, I thought he did a pretty good job. I was having good thoughts about the trip again, until he told us we were going to sleep under the stars that night. And work on developing a good team vibe. NO TENTS!" *UH-OH, another real BAD SIGN!"* I thought. This is July in Illinois where the mosquitoes can carry you away at night. If I had my car, I would have rock and rolled at this point. And I bet everyone else thought the same. That's probably why he drove us all over in his van. We were his captives. Good thing I brought insect repellent, but I didn't bring my mosquito head net which he talked about in the equipment talk. It was a little late now I thought. I also recalled at this point seeing a sign that said no overnight camping as we came into the forest preserve. I said, *"Hey Tuck what about the sign I saw about no camping allowed in the forest preserve?"* Tuck replied, *"Don't worry; I got a special permit for us to camp."* I thought, *"Yeah Right!"*

I looked around and noticed a lot of our crew did not look too happy about this development. Tuck said, *"I want you to separate and find a place to lay your sleeping bag for the night."* I thought, *"There is going to be a lot of scared people who aren't going to get a lot of sleep tonight."* After drenching myself with lots of insect repellent I found a nice quiet spot, on a wide part of the trail, and laid my pad and sleeping bag down snuggled in and tried to sleep. The insect repellant didn't seem to work at all and the buzzing in my ears was driving me crazy. The only thing that worked was putting my head completely in my bag and closing it. Then the thoughts of suffocation came roaring into my head, with images of being found cooked in a down bag on a hot summer night. And dead in the morning. It was not a good night! The only good news, if you are an optimist, is that it didn't rain.

At this point, you can imagine that I was really having doubts about going on this trip. Remember, everyone was supposed to bring their own food. Luckily, I had brought enough but can't say that everyone else did. You can imagine what was going through everyone's heads at this point. When I got up early the next morning, I noticed that everyone was up and none of us were happy campers, except maybe for surviving in our sleeping bag inferno's. Tuck created these vibes. And a lot of us were putting him on the hot seat. He said, *"This weekend is to develop team work, and make sure all of you can handle the conditions on the trip."* I asked, *"So we're not taking tents on the trip."* Tuck replied. *"Yes, don't worry, we'll have good tents for our trip."* People, I think kind of bought this. I did not, and thought *"OH BOY!"*

Then he said, *"We were now going to start some team building."* UH OH! He tied us all together with rope and we began walking or I should say stumbling through the woods. Lots of fun! Yeah Right! Then he said, *"Not bad. Let's try it with blind folds on."* I thought, *"Double OH Boy!"* What a blast we were all having, falling, and crashing into everything. Being a wise ass, I said, *"Hey Tuck, when are we going to practice blind fold canoeing?"* He just looked at me with no reply and may have realized then that I could be trouble. Even we Swamp Rats didn't do such foolish things and I suspected that Tuck had to have been a boy scout, probably a bad one, which us Rats had eaten for lunch. We continued, for the rest of the day with more wonderful team-building events. I was having even more doubts about the trip. And now, I understood why Bill didn't want to go on this weekend orientation. *"That rat fink, he should have warned me,"* I thought!

We walked back to the parking lot, tired from lack of sleep, hungry with not enough food, to get a ride back to our cars. I spied a ticket on the windshield of his van, obviously from the park ranger. Tuck quickly grabbed it and put it in his pocket. I said innocently, *"What was that Tuck?"* He replied, *"Just a thank you note from the Park Ranger for us picking this Park."* I looked at him funny and replied, *"Yeah Right."* I think Tuck may have gotten some of the bad vibes from our group. You think!! At the end, he said, *"Thanks for coming. You all did great and I think you all will do fine on the trip. See you in a couple weeks at the planetarium."* I thought, *"Maybe not me, because I might not be going. Hope I can get my deposit back."*

I talked a little with stepdad Bob and stepson Mark who lived in Rockford, about the trip before leaving for home. They, like me, had their doubts about the trip. They said, "*What do you think of Tuck?*" I said, being diplomatic, "*I don't know, this weekend seemed kinda weird to me and not necessary.*" Ben replied," *I agree. We're also thinking of pulling out.*" I said, "*Me too, but my friend, who was not here, that rat fink, had gone with Tuck before and said he was great.*" Bob continued, "*Well we'll probably go but we are going to drive our own car. We will be happy to drive you down to the Planetarium to meet Tuck.*" I said, "*Thanks.*" We exchanged numbers and said we would call if either of us dropped out and set a time to meet. I then went in and asked the people at the Clock Tower Inn if I could leave the car there for a couple of weeks. They said, "*Sure people do it all the time.*"

I called Bill Sunday night as soon as I got home and related the happenings of the weekend. And had serious doubts about the wisdom of going on the trip. He just laughed and said "*SO.*" I said, "*You asshole, why didn't you tell me what was going to happen?*" He was upbeat about the whole thing and claimed innocent knowledge of what was going to happen on our orientation weekend and he really had been busy. I said, "*REALLY.*" He really wanted me to go and said it would be great, but I was not yet convinced and told him I would have to think about it. Remember how I got the boot from the farm. And had a dead line to be out the end of July, and unfortunately, as the story unfolds, this was a deciding factor in making the decision to go on the trip. I planned to move to a trailer park with campground and it would save me a couple of weeks of rent. Being fugal, or maybe cheap, I decided, with lots of reservations, to go.

PLANETARIUM

I met Ben and Mark at the Clock Tower Inn at 11:30 Saturday morning in Rockford. They were very nice and had a great half hour machine going talking about the great adventure we were about to embark. We got there in plenty of time before the scheduled meeting time of 1:00pm. Everyone else was there, including my friend Bill who was very happy I chose to go on the trip. But no Tuck, big surprise! Who was there was Tuck's girlfriend Jan, and the other guide Mike, who we met at the orientation, who were both very nice. We all settled in and got to know each other a little better. There was Lyn, who was in college and had been on a backpack trip with Tuck, Sara, who was a little older, worked in a factory, and was a greenhorn, Larry an older man, probably younger than I am now and that ain't old. Let me try it again. Larry, a not so old man, who seemed sensible, also had been backpacking with Tuck. Ben and Mark, the step dad and son team, who never did anything like this before. And Mary, who was very friendly, and also inexperienced, Bill, and I.

We waited, and waited and waited and finally at about 6:30, to a choir of cheers, Tuck finally made the scene. He was driving his 15-passenger van and was pulling a trailer of Grumman aluminum canoes. Hooray! He said he had a problem getting the canoes, which I found out later he rented from a Boy Scout troop. *"I just knew it."* They probably had the same reservations that I had about trusting him. I didn't know it yet, just how right this sentiment would turn out to be. We packed or I should say crammed all our stuff in the trailer and van, which took another hour. And off we went, way behind schedule.

Bill and I were seated in back of the bus with Lyn and Mary. Mary and I were in the way back seat, which was nice because it was all the way across the back. I didn't realize yet just how nice. The plan was to drive straight through to Canada, so we were in for some real quality time on this bus crammed full of people and gear. Mary said, *"This is the first time I've done anything like this. How about you?"* I said, back to my hotshot self, *"Yeah, I have done a lot of paddling and I am only going on this trip, because of my friend Bill."* She said, *"Oh that's great. It is nice to have some experienced people on the trip."* I continued with more. *"Blah, blah, and blah"* and we were getting along famously. To my great surprise I felt a hand on my thigh and then? You know life is strange. I was a 26-year-old unattached male who spent a lot of time, like most normal males of my age, looking for a little love. So here I am, on a bus crammed full of people, sitting next to a woman with lascivious intentions. I thought, *"Why here"* and tried to resist. Yeah Right! It is the middle of the night and everyone else was sound asleep or so I thought. The Karma God must be stepping in after the, you know Florida trip where, you know what happened or didn't happen. Well, all I have to say, the rest of the night was interesting and something one never forgets. It was kind a like being in the "Mile High Club", but this was the "Crowded Big Van Club." The next day nobody seemed the wiser to our shenanigans. We tried to be quiet and I guess it worked, or everyone was just being nice!

CANADA

Par for the course, we got lost a few times before we crossed the border, but not surprisingly, we had trouble at the border. Tuck had packed a ton of food, with a lot being fresh, which is frowned upon when entering into another country. And after, what seemed like hours, and Tuck paying tariff money for all the food, they finally let us in. It was already late afternoon, and we were falling even farther behind schedule. We pushed on toward Cochrane, the ending point of our trip where we would return by train from Moosinee, a town located on James Bay. James Bay, the southernmost bay in the bigger Hudson Bay, which is part of the artic ocean.

Tuck's plan was to find someone in Cochrane to drive his rig back from our starting point at Mattice, which was 25 miles west of Cochrane on Rt. 11. It was getting late and we needed a place camp. Tuck decided to head out of town to try and find one. I wondered why he didn't ask somebody in town where we could camp. No luck, Tuck just kept driving and driving and we were soon lost. We came upon a farm and Tuck wisely decided to stop and ask directions. Oops! We are in Quebec and Tuck cannot understand anything the Quebec woman was saying, because she was speaking French, and even if she spoke English, which she probably did, the Quebec people, as we later found out, just would not. We continued with our quest and finally found an open field to camp, which was not the greatest but we were happy to get out of the damn van. It was now almost dark, and nobody, except Bill and I, because I brought my tent not trusting Tuck, knew how to set up tents. We were all starving, not having eaten anything since lunch. To make matters worse, my love interest now wanted to share our tent, which of course Bill wanted no part of and I concurred, thinking, *"What the heck did I get myself into."* She said, *"I want sleep in your tent."* I said, *"I don't think this would be a wise idea."* She said, *"Why not?"* I replied, *"What would everyone think and what about your tent mate Lyn? She may get scared sleeping alone."* This went on for a while, and I soon realized, that this girl is a lot too crazy for me. Unhappily, she finally agreed. This made for a tense and not so perfect night of camping, but we made do.

The next day, with the help of a compass, which I had on me, and finally finding an Ontarian to help us, we made it back to Cochrane. Tuck finally found a driver in a local tavern. He was a young Canadian about our age, to drive his rig back after dropping us off in Mattice for the beginning of our trip and off we went to Mattice. All the time he was looking for a driver for his van, I was thinking, Ben drove also so we could use his car to do the shuttle. We could simply drive the van to the put in, unload everything, then drive the rig to Cochrane followed by Ben who would then drive Tuck back after parking his rig at the train station. What's up with that? We wasted a whole lot of time trying to find a driver and probably could have camped at the put in?

At this point, with the comedy of errors, you can understand that I and probably everyone else was really beginning to worry about the wisdom of going on this trip. We were supposed to leave at 1:00 on Saturday but didn't leave till about 7:00 that night. We got stuck at the border because of all the fresh food that Tuck had brought. We got lost and spent lots of time trying to find a camp on Sunday. Tuck spent most of the morning Monday trying to find a driver, we didn't need, and we have a 200-mile trip planned with about 12 days to complete it. There was an obvious lack of planning for this trip, but at this point, our options were limited! Through the years, and even then, I knew how important a good plan was. Without a good plan, the chance of success is very slim.

When we arrived at Mattice, Tuck was having concerns, rightly, about being behind schedule. Duh! There was a dirt tract, on the east side of the river, which he thought we could drive on to take some miles off our trip. Little did he know that there was an actual road on other side of the river, which was way better, and could have shaved about 20 miles off the trip, and of course, he never checked? There is that plan thing again. It was a little rough at first, but soon turned into a dirt track, where we should have stopped. Not Tuck, on we went and, you guessed it, we soon were stuck. Real stuck. "*Oh boy!* I know now, from a life of dealing with canoes and trailers, that when you are stuck with a trailer the wise move is to empty and unhook the trailer, get the vehicle unstuck, and then move the trailer which is really not heavy when unloaded. Tuck, being young, dumb and full of XXX did not have this wisdom. He said, "*All of you get out and push.*" Some of us got behind the van and some behind the trailer. He gave her the gun and we instantly got covered in mud, And we looked like a bunch of gingerbread man cookies. Of course, the van didn't move and was even more stuck. He then yelled, "*Somebody get on the tongue of the trailer and jump up and down for traction.*" Can you guess what dump ass volunteered? You guessed it. This dumb ass. I yelled back. "*When you feel me jump give her the gas and ease her out, so don't floor it.*" If I weren't so young and dumb, I would not have volunteered to do this, because the possibility of being run over by the trailer is huge. Yep, you know what is coming next. He floored her and the trailer, and truck flew forward, and only by the shear good grace of God, I caught myself and didn't get run over. I thought, *"Not good, as my heart was racing wildly."* I felt extremely lucky, then screamed back at Tuck. *"What the F*** are you doing? I told you to ease her out. You almost ran me over!"* He didn't respond at all. I was having lots of apprehension now. A few years later, the opportunity to do a similar dumb move came up, only this time it was with a tractor pulling a tree that got stuck, and I smartly declined to get involved which would have killed me, so there is one up side to this event; I did learn something.

We soon came to a clearing, which would make a not good, but adequate camp, and Tuck wisely decided to camp. We then began to unload the truck and trailer, and with horror, I realized that nothing had been organized or packed at all. Good thing our Canadian driver, was good-natured, because he blew the rest of his day helping us. He told me he could not believe what he was seeing. He said, *"what a mess eh"* when he saw none of the food had been packed at all, and I replied, *"what a nightmare eh?"* It was just a huge pile of fresh, dehydrated and dried food. Tuck's girlfriend, and the help of everyone, started to try to make some sense out of this big pile of food. Having been down this road before, and now after a life of planning and packing food for trips, I realized how absurd this was. The hardest part of any trip is planning and packing the food. Even then, having several trips under my belt, I remembered with apprehension, all those other trips where we messed up planning the food and ended up starving yelling, "cheeseburger, cheeseburger" and eating raw carp! My worries grew. Things, with plenty of hands involved, were beginning to take shape. That is when our new Canadian came to the rescue and said *"Eh want a little something"*? *"This is just what the doctor ordered,"* I thought. Bill and I just couldn't refuse and said *"Yeah Eh."* We managed to have a little discrete party, which consisted of XXXXXX. Remember the thing about mothers!! Well, just let your imagination run free and figure it out.

That blew Tuesday, and nobody got anybody up early on Wednesday. We ate breakfast at about 11:00am. I knew that we had to be at Moosonee to catch the train back and thought, *"Man we had 200 miles, less a little bit to paddle, and time was running out."* Then Tuck announced, *"it's time to get in the water and practice paddling."* OH Boy", I thought. *"Why didn't we spend the orientation weekend working on canoe skills? Probably because Tuck was too cheep to rent canoes and a trailer for the day. We are already behind schedule and have not even started our trip!"* Of course, Bill and I were going to paddle together, and the rest of the partners were determined. So, we dragged our canoes to a spot just off shore. The river seemed really low, with lots of rocks, but still had some powerful current. Tuck immediately called upon Bill and me, who of course had acted like canoe hot shots, to show us how it was done. Tuck said," *Why don't you guys go out and play a little in the rapids and show us how it is done."*

So, Bill and I got in the canoe and, *"Man this is some powerful current"* I screamed as we tried to do the back ferry, and other stuff, we had seen George Steed do. He made it look easy but things were not going well at all, and once again, we proved that we were not the hotshots that we thought we were, and soon crashed. Tuck proceeded to ask the rest of our crew if they had ever paddled any whitewater. Yikes! Nobody had! I'm looking at the river and knew this was going to be something else. As I look back at this trip, I am even more mortified than I was then. Having taught whitewater paddling for 30 years, I realize how little Tuck knew about paddling and the foolishness of this trip. He gave us a few basic stokes to learn and we banged around for a couple of hours not learning much at all, but we were all excited and off we went, getting stuck on rocks almost immediately. *"Good thing the river is low or somebody may get killed,"* I thought. Tuck of course never thought to check this. With of our complete lack of canoe skills somebody could get hurt even with the low water.

The canoes were heavy with all the fresh food, and Tuck even had a rider in one boat. Even in my stupidity back then, I knew how dumb this practice is. *"Really, why not just throw a couple of 80lb sand bags in a canoe for some dead weight? You never know when you might need sand,"* I thought. If you remember we had already learned this lesson well on earlier trips. Way earlier. The good news was Bill and I put into practice our canoe skate boat method that we had invented on the South Fork of the Flambeau. It worked well, but there were endless rock gardens of rapids, so we paddled little, and walked a lot. We paddled to about 8:00pm and found a place to camp. We had managed to eek out about five miles and felt good about our progress. We were all tired and hungry. And it would soon be dark.

There is a lot to do to when you set up camp for the night. First, you have to pull up and secure your canoe and gear by putting it in a location that if a storm comes rolling in you will not be left without a boat, life jacket or paddle. You can see the wisdom of this practice. Then a smart person looks for a flat place to pitch their tent, keeping in mind wind direction, possible snorers, and in our case not too close to the nymphomaniac woman I have been trying to discourage. I can remember many a time sliding down a hill or rolling into one's unhappy partner. You also have to consider, dips, sharp stuff, hills and all that might cause you a night of discomfort and not sleeping well. On one previous trip we set up our tent on a nice little island not realizing it was infested with ants. The hungry little red ants that had eaten everything on the island and now wanted to eat us. It was a case of ecology gone horribly wrong. It was not the best of nights. Another time we found a nice flat spot to put up our tent not realizing that it was where all the water drained when it rains and woke up floating. What a way to start your day!

On this trip, none of us had the comfortable thermorest mattress that we use today. A thermorest mattress, for those of you who do not know about them, is a mattress that consists of an open foam core with a waterproof cover. It is like combining an air mattress and a foam pad. The air part is for comfort, the foam insulates you from the ground, which will suck the heat right out of you, making for a cold night. I once tried one of those big inflatable air beds, early on when we were building our resort, and froze my little buns off, because you are sleeping on air, which does not insulate you at all. A thermorest mattress is self-inflating, warm and comfortable. Thermorest, made by Cascade Design, was the original pad. Now there are a lot of knock offs around because their patent has expired. These would have been nice on the Missinaibi River, because it runs through the Canadian Shield. When the glaciers retreated, they ripped up the ground leaving exposed granite behind, making the "Canadian Shield Country." Lots of campsites in Shield Country are on granite. Unfortunately, we did not have these but only solid foam backpacker's pads, which are warm but not very comfortable. Rock is hard!!

It is a good idea to put up a line to dry any clothes. And in our case this night there was no need because it was getting dark. Also, if there is any threat of rain, a tarp would be a great idea. I can right a whole book just on hanging tarps. Cooking and eating in the rain are not my idea of a good time. Firewood has to be collected, a fire pit dug or fire ring made, and then a fire has to be built. A campfire provides warmth, peace of mind, and is a wonderful medium for excellent stories. Water also has to be collected, filtered and treated. It is tempting in the far north, with beautiful clear water, to drink it directly out of the river or lake. Don't do it! There are naturally occurring amoeba called giardia that are found in beaver and moose poop! Giardia lambia is about 2 microns, so you need a filter that will filter down to one micron. Then the meal has to be organized, cooked and served. And after the meal all the dishes need to be washed well to prevent getting sick and then the food has to be protected from animals, small and large. We double bag everything and put it in a waterproof bag or box. We then hang it in a tree if possible. The best prevention from having any problems with animals is to keep a clean camp. Never leave food around after a meal, clean your dishes well, and burn all your food scrapes.

There is also a lot of dangerous stuff that you need to consider when in the wilderness and in camp. One of the biggest is preventing a bad cut, help is far away. Using an ax is one of the worst methods of cutting firewood. A saw is much safer and more effective. Going in water without shoes is another real danger, and as you may remember, I discovered this early on when George cut his foot bad on one of our first canoe outings. Wearing shorts, which offer no protection from a fall, sharp sticks, insects and sun is also a bad idea.

A camp stove can also be dangerous. A common small back packer stove or canoe camp stove uses Colman fuel and has a system of pumping air to provide pressure to the fuel. Colman fuel is very flammable, even more so than gasoline. This above knowledge will help you understand why things did not go exactly as planned on our fist night on the river.

Jan, Tuck's girlfriend, took charge of getting the meal together. Tuck got the firewood together and started the fire. Mike the other guide, was trying to take on by himself all the other chores that needed to be done, with the rest of us standing around doing nothing. I have learned through the years that if you ask people to help and give them direction they will happily jump right in and get to work. This was not happening; a few were trying to do the majority of the work, rushing around trying to beat the dark. I learned these things through experience and now know that making camp late and rushing to get all these chores done is a recipe for disaster. This is what led to our first accident.

Jan was trying to get all the food together and she asked Lyn to get the stove going. Lyn was a go getter, but had no clue as to how to do this, but she tried. It can be a tricky proposition, and if you don't pump up the stove just right it can flare up and even explode, and that is just what happened. The stove flared up and vroom! The stove survived but Lyn got a nasty burn. Not good! She was a real trooper. We finally got the food together and everyone got fed. It was now dark which made the rest of the chores for the evening even harder.

It is now Wednesday and in Tuck fashion we did not get breakfast done and boats loaded until about 11:00am. We were all determined and made some tough miles through the endless rock gardens, and then came to our first portage around a fall. Tuck was really pushing now, because I think he realized what we were in for and was overwhelmed himself. He was relying on his boy scout training, which was not the best, and showed us how one person could carry a canoe tying two paddles together to make a crude yoke. A 17' Grumman canoe weighs around 75 lbs and is a heavy load for an inexperienced person or anyone to carry with a crude yoke or otherwise.

We are rushing now trying to make up time. Larry was wearing hiking boots, which do not have good traction on wet rocks, to do the portage and fell on the wet granite at the landing, dislocating his thumb. This is our second accident in two days; a real bad sign. He was the oldest one in our group and handled the trauma well, but he needed medical attention and was in a lot of pain. We had passed an access point with the realization that we could have avoided all those endless rock gardens by starting our trip at this access point, which had a good road leading to it. There were a couple of locals fishing there who said there were even a couple of more access point down river. Tuck decided that he and Mike would paddle Larry back to the access in the hope that the people fishing were still there and they could help get Larry to a doctor. He said," Jeff, you and Jan take the group down river, find a place to camp, and then wait for us at the next access." I said, *"No sweat, don't worry we'll be fine."* And up river they went.

We were making good time and after traveling for couple of hours, we camped. It was earlier than usual and, with a little organization and everyone helping, things went well. Having been a teacher for 6 years, I knew how to motivate people. When everyone in a group works as team, it develops a great environment of positive waves. We had a great relaxing and fun evening. Everyone agreed, that night, that an early start would help us make up some time, and everyone went to bed a happy camper, maybe except Mary, who I was still resisting.

We got up at 6:00am with everyone helping with food and breaking camp, and got on the river at about 8:00am. We were moving fast and spirits were high. At about ten we arrived at the second access point, and waited for Tuck and Mike to show up. Mike and Tuck showed up surprised that we had made so much progress at about 11:00, at which point we thought we would head out and continue to make up time. NOT!

GROUP REAM OUT

Tuck was obviously pissed and put us in a circle, with him in the middle and began to read us the riot act. He had been singling out Mark, Ben's stepson, on the trip before and was staring at him the whole time he was yelling at us. Tuck said, *"Everyone here has to get their act together. We cannot have these accidents and everyone has to work a lot harder and listen to me. Some of you should never have even been on this trip and are nothing but dead weight,"* and so forth. This went on for about an hour, and I was not surprised that the mood had changed from great, to a real bummer. We had been working as a team, had made great time and things were going great. I thought, *"What a dumb F*** Tuck was; he should be congratulating us not giving us shit."* Suddenly Mark snaps, he jumps up and yells, *"You F***** who do you think you are? You are nothing but a dumb f**** and I'm going to kick your ass."* He then pulls out a big hunting knife he had on his belt, and goes after Tuck. OH BOY! Ben, his Stepdad, yells, *"Mark stop!"* and grabs Mark with some of us close behind. After a short tense struggle, we manage to take away the knife. I know I was thinking, *"way to go Mark"*, but really; a knife fight on a river trip! Ben said, *"we have had enough of your bull crap you f******* bastard. What the hell is the matter with you? "Everything was going great until you came back. We're through taking your shit,* *you incompetent bastard and we're out a here."* Tuck yelled, "great!" They grabbed their packs and water bottles and left.

Jan implored, *"Tuck you can't let them walk out, these are city boys and it's a twenty-mile hike with no tent, and no food."* Tuck said, *"They made their own decision, F*** them!"* Luckily, their car was left by the road where we put-in, but none us were confident that they would make it out. Smartly they grabbed their water, but they were going to get real hungry real soon.

BEN AND MARK BRAVE THE WILD

Here is the story that Ben related to me, when I called him, after the trip. Ben said *"I can't believe how pissed off we both were. How did you keep so calm? You were the only one who knew what the XXXX you were doing. We should have made that rat bastard Tuck walk back.*

At first, we were high on the adrenalin from the fight but after about an hour, we realized, what the hell we had gotten ourselves into. We had never been alone in the wilderness before. There was not a soul around and every time we heard any sound both Mark and I were sure it was a bear. We thought that we would run into somebody and get a ride. But nothing, there was nothing but a lot of trees, endless trees. You remember how hot it was when we left. We only had two quarts of water and drank most of that the first day. You can't imagine how thirsty, tired and hungry we were the second day. I wish we had packed lighter those damn packs weighed a ton. We had no idea how long it would take for us to walk out, and we both got scared that we wouldn't make it. Then the sun started to go down and the mosquitoes were biting the crap out of us. We had some repellant but it didn't seem to help much. Then it got dark and it soon got cold;

really cold. We just sat there, huddled in our sleeping bags up against a tree. It was the worse F**** night of my life. I was sure we were going to die, and kept thinking what a F**** bastard that Tuck was and wished that I had let Mark kill him." I said, "*You don't really mean that do you?*" He said "*Yeah, you're right, Mark would have gotten in trouble.*" He continued, "*Anyway, it finally started to get light. We had slept fitfully, feeding every F**** mosquito in Canada. We were dead tired, but we had made it through the night. You can't believe how awful it was to begin walking again with the awful blisters we had on our feet. But you know what?*" "*No*" I said. He replied, "*We were so hungry and tired we were no longer scared; let the F***** bear eat us if he wants. We just kept walking, with thoughts of Cheeseburgers and beer on our minds.* I said, "*I can relate to that, a couple of times on canoe trips we ran out of food. Did you and Ben chant Cheeseburgers! Cheeseburgers!*" "*No*" he said, "*We were too F***** tired. We just kept walking and around three o'clock, we came to our car.*" "*I could not believe it. We made it. It was the happiest moment of my life. We threw our packs into the car, started her up, and headed to Chochrane in a quest for cheeseburgers and beer.*" We both then commiserated on what a dick wad Tuck was. He said he had called Tuck and demanded their money back, and did not get much sympathy from him at all, which pissed him off even more. He said, "*I'm going to sue that incompetent bastard and make him pay for what he did to us.*"

BACK ON THE RIVER

We started with two riders in the canoes, and Tuck's plan was to leave Ben and Mark's canoe behind, so we would still have a rider. Here is where I let Tuck know how dumb that was and offered to solo a canoe. I said "Let me solo Ben and Mark's canoe, which will give us no rider and make for much lighter canoes and better progress" Tuck said, *"No we can't do that, you always have to have a rider."* I said, *"The canoe will probably be stolen"* Tuck said, "It's *not my canoe it's the boy scouts canoe*" I said, "Aren't *you responsible for the canoe and we will be much lighter as a group and make better time"* and so forth. Then everyone in the group jumped in on my side and Tuck unhappily relented.

I certainly, not by any means, was an expert solo paddler, but was enjoying the challenge. Being lighter, we were making good time, although the mood of the group was not good after the unbelievable fiasco earlier. We soon came upon the last access point, the point of no return, and who do find sitting there. Oh my God, it's none other than Larry! Everyone screamed, "*LARRY!*" He told us, *"After I got my thumb put back into place I found a guy, Pete, in Hearst, where the clinic was, with a four-wheel truck who said he knew the road up the west side of the river. I gave him a few bucks, and he happily brought me here."* He introduced us to Pete who was still there who said, "*I fish this area and hoped that we could beat you here, but thought it would be a good idea, if I stuck around in case we missed you eh.*" Larry thanked his Canadian friend, and the coolest part was, we now have an even group, and was secretly relieved that I didn't have to solo the remainder of the trip.

The mood again changed to the positive, with the arrival of Larry, and we traveled a good ten more miles and found a nice camp. One of the problems when traveling with a group of 10 is finding a big enough place to camp. The group knew the routine now with everyone doing their jobs and working together. The camp went up fast, and everyone again was in a festive mood. We had a good meal, made a big fire, and then the shit hit the fan. Well, not really but kina off. Lyn suddenly got sick. She got real sick with stuff coming out both ends. That's the shit hitting the fan part. The next morning, she was a little better, but the mood again had swung south, and in Tuck fashion, we did not get an early start, but finally, off we went. Going was a lot slower that day as other people in our group started to get ill, and all were looking forward to getting to Thunder House Falls where we hoped it was good camping.

Finally, after an arduous day of paddling through more rock gardens, we hear the awesome roar of the falls, and as we approached carefully, we could see that the river narrowed and the current began to speed up. We did not see a portage trail but knew it had to be soon or over the thirty-foot falls, we would go. "*Holy crap it would be easy to be sucked right over this fall,*" I thought. Being scared, we used extreme caution approaching the falls and saw the portage trail, which in my view was way to close to the falls. It turned out that I was right about that, because later I heard a man had died here, not long ago, missing the portage and indeed, went flying over the falls. "*This would not be a good way to die,"* I thought. With a sigh of relief, we managed to get every one out safely and all our boats secured. We are now looking at a long portage, about a mile, which started with a steep hill. I thought, *"This is going to be a real pull."* We rigged

our canoe paddles for a yoke and struggled up the trail. I was young and fit, but man I thought., *"I don't know if I can make it up this hill and to the other side and how stupid it is to carry this heavy canoe alone."* About halfway thru the portage, we came to a bunch of nice campsites. The pack mules, in Tuck fashion, were double hauling the big heavy packs. That's' right, one on the front and one on the back, but luckily, they could drop their packs at these campsites, cutting their portage in half. Us young, macho and stupid canoe mules bravely continued on, beating ourselves up, to the end of this tortuous portage!

There was a guy in a C1 already camped there. A C1 looks like a kayak but you kneel inside instead of sitting. His name was Jack and the first thing I asked him was about his choice of boats. Being a lot smaller than a canoe, it is not the boat of choice for a two-hundred-mile two-week trip down the Missinaibi. Jack than began to relate his story. He said, *"I am a whitewater canoe instructor from Pennsylvania and was paddling with a group of ten people in canoes, who like us, had lots of trouble with the low water and endless rock gardens. They quickly got discouraged around the second access point and gave up. He said their plan was to walk out, which was not his idea of a good time. He had his own car that was at Hearst and wanted to finish the trip. He realized that going it alone was dangerous and hoped that a group would come along that he could tag along with."* He said, *"I have been camping here for a couple of days and was waiting for someone to show up and hopped now that he could get connected with us for the rest of the trip."* I thought," *Great, here's a guy that has his shit together."* I told Jack that Tuck was the leader and he had to ask him.

LAY OVER DAY

We set up our camp and more of us were starting to get sick and Lyn, who was the first one to get sick on Thursday, was now feeling better. Bill and I were still feeling fine and invited Jack to our camp to meet everyone. He hung with us for the night and got along fine with everyone, but had not yet asked Tuck if he could join us on the trip. In the middle of the night, our camp sickness hit Bill, who got violently ill, losing stuff from both ends. Then it hit me in the morning. Not Good! It came on like gangbusters and man was I sick. I now believe that we all suffered from food poisoning that was caused by the fresh food Tuck had brought, or from inadequate cleaning of the cook gear or both. This was another great learning experience; one I do not want to repeat. I never, unless it is a short trip where we can bring a cooler, bring anything fresh on a canoe trip. I also make sure that the washing of the dishes takes place promptly after we eat and are washed thoroughly and rinsed well.

You remember the really friendly girl on the trip who I was trying to avoid, and had accomplished this successfully so far? Well, there I was deliriously sick lying in my tent, with her now taking advantage of my helpless soul. And whispering in my ear all the wonderful things she wanted to do to me when I got better. *OH*

BOY! I have to admit though that there are worse ways to spend a day being sick.

Saturday night I started feeling much better, and was quickly informed that the group was going to paddle the 30 miles up stream and walk out the rest of the way. We had walked many of those 30 miles of rock garden low rapids and the thought of going back upstream against that was absurd. I immediately went to talk to Bill who informed me that this was true, and then went to find Jack.

Jack said, *"While you were sick, a Canadian gentleman, Pasquale, and his lady friend had arrived, and he had done the trip before solo. I talked to him about the rest of the trip and he said that we had gone through the hardest part and would have no trouble making it to Moose Crossing by Thursday, where we could catch the train up to Moosinee and then ride back to Cochrane on Friday. All we had to do was get up early every day, get on the water by no later than 6:30 and put in about 12 hours of paddling a day. He did it solo in about 4 days and he said we should have no problems."* "Cool," I thought. I then said, *"Great I'm in; all we have to do is talk the rest of the group into it."* I then went to find Pasquale and asked him if he would tell this to our group, which he agreed to do.

I went and found Tuck and told him what I learned, but he was very reluctant, which I didn't understand. *"Didn't he want to finish the trip I thought?"* I said to him, *"Hey Tuck, we all paid good money to go on this trip and I for one would want a refund if we are unable to complete it as planned."* That changed his mind and he got the group together right after dinner.

Pasquale came through with a very convincing speech about how we had gone through the worst and now it would be easy and so forth. I learned a very important lesson that day, which has helped me be a successful guide through out the rest of my life.

A group can be a powerful force, capable of doing amazing things or it can be an unmovable force capable of making incredibly wrong decisions. Once a group turns south there is no bringing it back, especially when fear takes over. Through the years of leading many trips, I have seen people fail in completing their trips. I ask my canoe students all the time what they the think is the reason these people fail to make their planned trips? Few people ever get the answer correct. Fear, a very powerful emotion, takes over is the reason.

When we get afraid, logic goes right out the window. I have witnessed many a paddler going upstream in some incredibly horrible conditions, and have tried many times, unsuccessfully, to convince them of the errors of their ways, which is why Pasquale was not successful in convincing our group. Even in our canoe livery business, on the Headwaters of the Wisconsin River, we used to see this often. The Headwaters of the Wisconsin is a beautiful little wild stream that is not boring but not threatening either. It has a good current, but still people convince themselves that they are lost and turn back upstream and go to where they know, because they are afraid. We prevent this by simply warning them not to do this, because they are not lost and will come to their takeout. Problem solved.

Our group was at that bad negative place and you cannot blame them for that, with the lack of leadership and total ineptness of our guide. They were afraid. They wanted out no matter how hard it was going to be. I had already completed many excellent adventures, as you know, and had some wisdom and trusted Pasquale, and wanted to finish this trip. And now all I had to do was to convince Bill.

Bill said he wanted to go but was still in the clutches of the group. I told him that he talked me into this trip, even after that awful orientation weekend that he had skipped, and I wanted to finish what we had started. He finally said OK. I may have also threatened violence; you know that fear thing can work for you sometimes. HA! Jack was way up for it, now only Tuck stood in our way.

Tuck said," *I can't let you take the canoe. I rented them from the scouts.*" I said *"Come on, you were going to leave a canoe behind at that landing and you promised everyone that they we would get to Moosonee."* He said "Yeah so what." I said, *"Bill and I will want our money back if you don't let us go on."* He said, *"It would probably take us at least two or three days to go up stream and walk out and I guess I could take the group by train up to Moosonee and meet you on Thursday."* He said, *"You are responsible for the canoe and you better be there by Thursday."* I said, *"Great now we need to get some food."* We went through the food that we had left with Tuck and grabbed some. It was not the best but we wouldn't starve, and hoped we could supplement it by catching some fish. We had our own tent, sleeping bags, paddles and sleeping pads. Jack had cooking gear and food and so we were good to go. We packed everything, said our sad goodbyes, wished them luck and off we went Sunday morning, thinking, *"we have 5 days to make Moose Crossing or we are in some deep dew. No sweat."* I hoped!

ON OUR OWN

We were all very excited and felt relieved to be on our own. Jack immediately assessed our skill levels and began to train us as we traveled. Bill and I had paddled a lot together and knew a few basic strokes and both of us welcomed his training. Jack started by correcting the way we did our draw strokes and push away strokes. These strokes move the boat sideways, parallel to the current, without spinning. This works well in whitewater, because when the boat is broadside to the current, even a little bit, it grabs the canoe and pushes you to some place you may not want to go. Like into a big rock, where you pin the boat and wreck it. *"Been there done that!"* I thought. He also showed us the pry, an alternate stroke for the push away. We then worked on turning strokes; sweep, reverse sweep and cross draws. Learning these strokes, which I had seen George Steed do, gave us a level of control over the canoe that was incredible. We then began working on maneuvering techniques. First, Jack taught us how to ferry a canoe. This is a cool technique where you use the current to move the boat sideways, and you may even avoid hitting that big rock and wrecking the canoe. You start by back paddling to slow down the canoe, and then angle the canoe just right, catching the current while still back paddling, and the canoe moves sideways and not down stream. This is called a back ferry. You can do this very same maneuver by spinning the canoe around and paddling forward upstream. This is called a forward ferry. *"Very Cool,"* I thought. We then worked on eddy turns, which is a maneuver that takes advantage of eddies. An eddy is a place behind a rock, shore or whatever where the current is blocked. You can spin around behind the eddy and sit. This gives you time to scout the rapid, get you out of trouble, and aids greatly in getting you safely off the river. Jack also talked about reading the rapids and how current flows.

Later that day we came to our first rapid. Jack said, *"Ok here is your first test. You want to enter the rapid slowly by back paddling, pick your route by looking short and planning long, and remember GO SLOW. This will give you the time you need to react."* "OK," we said. He entered first and grabbed an eddy. I thought, *"He sure made it look easy."* We entered and started to back paddle right away and wow, we could stop the canoe even in this fast water. We saw a nice shoot that was to our left, so I angled the boat like he taught us and we moved right over." I thought, *"How cool is this? We're learning to paddle like George Steed and his partner, who blew me away with their skill on the Wolf River."*

I'm making this sound a lot easier than it was. We learned these techniques over the several days of the remainder of the trip, and have perfected them over a lifetime. However, it was a "WOW", and the joy of paddling went through the roof.

The first day we came to a gorge and pulled out at the portage trail. I think now, it is called Hell's Gate Canyon, but we didn't know that then. We hiked up a bit and scouted the rapid. Jack said this was too hard for our skill level but he thought that he may be able to handle it, but would portage his gear just in case. Bill and I did not have fond memories of portaging the canoe solo, and always before had done it with two people, which is easier and safer. The only reason we did it the other way was Tuck's macho insistence. What I do recommend highly for all heavy tandem tripping or whitewater canoes is to portage the boat backwards using the stern seat as a shoulder rest for the back

person, or even better, they can rest their shoulders in the narrow front gunnels of the canoe, with their head inside. The front person puts the very tip of the canoe on their shoulder. This reduces the weight to a very reasonable amount and with the tip of the canoe on the front person's shoulder, it offers great vision and maneuverability because the front person can move the canoe from shoulder to shoulder to help get around trees. The rule I always follow now; it is not important how fast you do a portage, but what you can do after a portage is what counts. Of course, early on this trip, if you recall, Larry had dislocated his thumb because he was rushing on a portage trail. This almost wrecked his trip.

We waited for Jack, and it seemed like it was taking forever and we started to get nervous. Because it was a gorge you could only see the beginning of the rapid and we had no way of seeing what was going on or helping Jack if he got in trouble. We had confidence in his ability, but we were still rightly nervous. Finally, visibly shaken, he showed up. He said, *"The rapid was much harder than I thought and I almost didn't make it. There was a big drop half way down where I had to eddy out and line the boat through, but it was intense and I almost lost control."* His CI had two stowed lines in the front and the back of about twenty feet in length. Jack used these lines to maneuver the boat from shore safely over the falls. He said *"next time if I could not see the entire rapid, I would just walk."* We said "GOOD IDEA."

We made great time in our first day of paddling. And even with a late start, because of food packing, calculated that we had traveled about 15 miles. We all knew what to do around camp and quickly got our tents set up, firewood, clothesline up and fire started. Now, we needed to figure out a meal. As a bonus Jack had caught some Walleyes and with the mismatch of things like canned tuna, macaroni and cheese, beans and so forth and with some of the stuff Jack had, made a pretty tasty meal. We knew we wouldn't eat gourmet but would not starve either. Our mood was great and we all felt confident that we had made the right decision to finish the trip.

We got up at first light the next day, had a simple breakfast of oatmeal and got on the water at 6:30, just as Pasquale had suggested. It was a beautiful morning with a misty fog over the water that soon burned away into a beautiful day. Bill and I were gaining skill by the hour and the rapids we were paddling took on a completely new dimension. And we're now playing in them and not just surviving them. What a blast!

Everything that Pasquale had described was proving to be true about the river. It had turned from an almost continuous string of rock garden rapids to a drop and pool river. A drop and pool river is where you have slower stretches of river between rapids, which are called drops. The river had good current in these quiet sections and we were making great time. We found another great place to camp that night after making an awesome twenty-five miles.

It was now Tuesday, and again at first light, we made a quick breakfast and got on the water at 6:30. We were taking no chances that we would miss the train at Moose Crossing at 6:00pm on Thursday. We had good weather our first couple of days but it then became overcast and looked like it might rain. The river was getting bigger as it marched toward Hudson Bay, and the space between rapids was getting longer and longer. It started to rain that afternoon, but with raincoats, it was not a problem. A little while later, we saw a moose and calf, which were not far away on the edge of the river. When you see these magnificent creatures in the wild, it is a real treat and reminds you just how awesome nature is. This was only the second time in my life that I had seen a moose, and was the first time for Jack, who was madly taking pictures, and Bill, who was searching for his camera missed the shot. Now that we were traveling in a small group, we were seeing a lot more wildlife. We saw eagles, muskrats, beavers, deer, and even a small bear. Life was just too good, even with the rain.

That night we had practice putting up the small tarp that Jack had brought. It was a tight fit, but we were warm and out of the rain. We had been sipping on a little whiskey that Jack had brought and began to talk about how great the trip had become. We wished both our groups, who had turned back, were here to share this with us. We couldn't imagine how the last couple of days for our group had been, pulling up stream twenty miles through those rock gardens and then walking out. We hoped they made it and were out. And we were anxious to hear the stories when we were reunited. Bill and I also wondered how Ben and Mark had fared with their twenty mile walk with only water and no food!

It was now Wednesday, and we had the routine down, again starting early. Through the years of doing canoe trips, it is always amazing how, with each passing day, it becomes better and better. I think this is because you get used to the simple life style that river travel provides. Life goes back to its simplest form, being fed, warm, having a nice place to camp, and the adventure of traveling the unknown. Once you get used to the routine it is a very enjoyable way to live, and you forget all those troubles and complications that modern living entails.

The river was now becoming large and the current was slowing, making paddling harder. "*UH OH! The wind is picking up,*" I shouted. Good thing we had started early, and had already made about 15 miles because we now know we would have to earn the last miles of the day. We were, unbelievably ahead of schedule, and camped a little early that day. And the weather had improved, Jack had caught more fish and we feasted. Not only were we not starving we were eating well. The only regret was not bringing a damn fishing pole. Jack was having all the fun. Well not all; if you have ever eaten freshly caught walleye, you know what a treat it is, and we were doing that everyday!

It was now Thursday and we had only about 10 miles to go and hoped we would not have the headwind that we had the day before. It was again misty in the morning and knew that odds were that we would have a great day. We noticed that when there was a lot of dew and fog in the morning it usually turns into a nice day because, the moisture was low. And when it was dry in the morning when the moisture was high, it rained. Checking for dew in the morning and predicting the weather is a great way to impress your friends with your weather prediction skills.

Every couple of hours throughout our trip we would stop so Jack could stretch his legs. I thought that kneeling in the small cramped cockpit of his boat had to be very hard on the legs and painful. It was impressive that he could make it that long. I didn't know just how painful, until he asked me if I wanted to try his C1 out. I stupidly said,*"sure."* First, it was a real bitch to get into the boat, and most importantly, it was not comfortable. Second, the boat was very tippy. I thought,*"How the heck did he keep this boat up right in the rapids?"* It didn't take long before I regretted my decision to try this boat from hell. *"Shit this ain't good,"* I thought and began to look for a place that I could escape this diabolical torture machine. I couldn't feel my legs and feet and knew I was in trouble. I spotted an island and bolted for it. When I got close and the water was shallow, I knew I wouldn't be able to get out, so I did the only practical thing. I tipped the boat over, and was like a beached whale, waiting for my legs to change from a couple pieces of wood to something useful. Meanwhile, Jack and Bill were laughing their asses off over my whale impersonation. When they made the scene the first thing, I asked Jack was, *"How in the hell do you do that?"* While laughing he said, *"I think you grow some new blood vessels after a while and it's not too bad."* Yeah right, I was never happier in my life to get back into our canoe. Bill, being the smart one, remember he didn't show up for the orientation weekend from hell, declined to give it a try.

"HOORAY!", we all cheered as we saw the bridge and train tracks that was Moose Crossing, which had nothing there, just as Pasquale had described it. We saw a path up a steep hill where we landed that led to the tracks and an obvious place where people had waited for the train. It was at about 2:00 pm, and we happily waited for the train to arrive.

MOOSONEE

The train came through as expected; we waved it down, loaded our stuff in a boxcar and were soon on our way to Moosonee. We were now a bunch of happy; very happy canoers. The trip had turned out to be just as Pasquale had described. We followed his suggestions and had no troubles. We were excited about being reunited with our friends and could not wait to hear the stories of their evacuations. We were looking forward to rubbing in how great our trip turned out and what they had missed. We expected them to be waiting for us when we pulled into the station. It was not like there were a lot trains coming into the station. There was exactly one. It came up one day and went back the next, at the same time each day.

We arrived expecting to see all our friends with smiles on their faces, congratulating us on our accomplishments. We looked around and Bill said, *"Where the heck are they?"* I said, *"I have no idea, but who knows what Tuck has them doing. Maybe they are paddling around the bay."* We bought our ticket for the next day and went on a quest to find them. There was not much to the town of Moosonee, but we soon found a café and you guessed it, cheeseburgers were on the menu! We all ordered, you guessed it, cheeseburgers, fries and a coke. There probably is a McDonald's there today, although I sure hope not.

We continued to explore the town, looking for our friends with no luck, and came to the conclusion that they must have come up earlier and would be waiting for us at the station in Cochrane. Jack said that he would treat us to a hotel room for the night. There was only a couple of choices, and they weren't the Ritz, but to us, it was heaven. We took our first hot showers in almost two weeks and had an actual bed to sleep in.

We spent the rest of the evening sipping whiskey, talking about how great the second part of our trip had been, and how lucky we were to run into Pasquale at Thunder House Falls. He had given us invaluable advice. We also talked about how unprepared both groups had been, especially ours in attempting to do a river like the Missinaibi. And reviewed all the things that went wrong which caused both groups to fail

First, there was a great lack of planning, and research. The Missinaibi is not a river for the novice paddler and wilderness tripper, which made it a bad choice for both groups. Tuck, our leader, had never done anything close to a trip like this. He did not have the wisdom or knowledge to realize this. Second, river levels are very important in planning a trip. The Missinaibi River in high water could be very dangerous, people could get hurt, and in low water, like what we experienced in the first part of the trip, would not be a walk in the park. Oh, excuse me; it would be a nightmare walk in Rock Garden Rapids Park. Third, nobody had the paddling skills to do this trip, except Jack, who was able to give these skills to us, which made for a great trip. Fourth, we now realized how important it was to start early, giving lots of time to deal with what the day may bring. And more importantly, to keep the positive attitude, which is so critical in completing a wilderness trip. Our group had gotten behind from the first day when Tuck was late and then everyday after that which lead to our group becoming afraid of not completing the trip, dying and whatever. This is why our group, except Bill and I turned back to paddle up those nightmare rock gardens and walk out twenty miles, even with the great advice

that Pasquale had given them. Fifth, fresh food on an extended canoe trip, with no refrigeration, can lead to people getting extremely ill, which everyone in our group did. And we were lucky that it was not worse than it was. In addition, fresh food is heavy, and heavy is not good for portaging or paddling and makes for more walking. Sixth, having three people in a canoe is not necessary and not good, for all kinds of reasons. Seventh, always bring fishing equipment when paddling on a wilderness trip. Having fresh fish to munch on is a delight. Eighth, never go on a wilderness trip lead by a dick wad "Tuck." Ninth, we all agreed that the second part of the trip was great, and that it was what a canoe trip was supposed to be. Last, but not the least, if you want to have great memories you have to have excellent adventures.

COCHRANE

It was a scenic and rewarding train ride back to Cochrane, in the glowing pride of completing a challenging wilderness trip. We arrived at the station in the early afternoon looking for our smiling group, awaiting us. UH OH! No group. *"What the hell, we thought! Where are they?"* I said, *"Maybe they are just running late,"* Bill said, *"Wouldn't be the first time."* We unloaded all our stuff from the train, and still no Tuck. The worry bug was eating at us hard. Bill said, *"Did that asshole leave us?"* Being an optimist, I said, *"Even Tuck can't be that big of an ass."* It was not long before we could no longer come to any other scary conclusion. That was exactly what he was. *"Son of a bitch what do we do now"* I said? Here we are stranded in Canada, with our two large duluth packs, complete with head bands for portaging, a 17-foot Grumman canoe and twenty-five dollars between us. I said, a real understatement, *"Not good."*

Jack lived in Pittsburg Pennsylvania and he very graciously said he would take us back to Chicago. With much relief we said *"Great."* Jack paid a Canadian to drive his car back to Cochrane from Mattice, and went to get it from the back parking lot. It took him about fifteen minuets to get back with his Volkswagen Bus and I noticed right away the loud knocking sound coming from the engine. Being a poor musician and experienced in working on many cars, I knew right then, that we were in real trouble. Jack's van was going to need some serious repairs. *"What now?"* we both exclaimed!

Bill and I started to hash out our options, which were not many. We knew there were no bus routes that came through here, and we checked to see if we could take the train back to Chicago, again no luck. Even if we found a way for us to get back, what about the canoe that we were responsible for? There was a phone booth, with a phone book, near by, and we checked to see how much it would cost to ship the canoe back. We soon found out it was very expensive and very hard to do. It did not take us long to scrap that idea! Jack had already gotten on the phone and found a mechanic that could repair his van, but it would take a week. We didn't have a week. I was a piano teacher and Bill taught high school in Chicago and we both had to get home. I remember my excellent adventure hitch hiking to Florida, and then said, *"Hitch hiking is the only option."* Bill said, *"Yeah I think you're right."* At this point, we felt responsible for the canoe, but you know Tuck had broken his promise and, Tuck, who obviously did not care about it or us, stranded us in Canada. *"What was he thinking that dick wad?"* We both thought. I think we were both in shock at this point and had a hard time believing that he could have done this to us. In our wildest dreams we would not have believed that Tuck was capable of this. Jack then said, *"I'll take the canoe back to Pittsburg with me and you or Tuck can come get it there."* That is when, I think we became resigned to our fate and became ready for another excellent adventure!

HITTING THE ROAD

Jack gave us a map of Canada. We decided it probably would be wise to stay on the Trans-Canada, RT. 11 Highway, because we thought there would be more traffic. By this time, it was already 8:00pm, when we put our best face on and our thumbs out, and waited. After about an hour of frustration, with many cars passing by, we decided we needed to try something else. Jack had been sitting near by, keeping us company, as we waited to be picked up. "*Cut a piece of cardboard and make a sign explaining what you ratty looking dudes are doing. You are a scary couple of people, and those huge packs don't help! What did you expect?*" Jack said. We wrote in big letters; PLEASE HELP. STRANDED CANOEIST NEED RIDE! That did the trick; it was not long, after saying our goodbyes and wishing Jack luck, before we were on are way heading west toward Thunder Bay.

Our first ride was a nice older couple who of course wanted to hear all about our adventures. I expected this after my adventure hitch hiking to Florida, and always provided a great half hour machine for the nice people who would pick us up. Bill and I had planned to share these duties, leaving one of us to get some shuteye. Of course, we had plenty to share about how we had gotten into this predicament. I think curiosity was the reason most people picked us up, and we did have a damn good story to tell.

They drove us for a couple of hours and let us out in their hometown. We had to wait awhile again but finally got picked up by a couple of guys heading to Thunder Bay. It was already dark and we were contemplating looking for someplace to sleep, when these two guys about our age stopped. They were partying hardy. And driving a Dodge Charger like my brother had. His was not a hot rod, but this Charger most definitely was a hot rod. Bill and I gave each other that, "I'm scared shitless look", as they burned rubber out of there. We were both very happy to be in the back seat as we contemplated a fiery crash. We figured it was better to die happy than scared and joined in on their party. They said they were going to visit a friend in Thunder Bay for a weekend of fun. Thunder Bay, being a Port town, offers lots of opportunites to have fun and get into lots of trouble. We were able to take turns sleeping which our party hosts hardly noticed.

We made great time to Thunder Bay, traveling at over 150 kms an hour. I knew that was fast and was trying to figure out just how fast. I learned on my other Canadian trips how to convert kilometers into miles, and knew this was fast. Let's see how fast I thought as I divided 150 by 5, which is 30 and then multiplied by 3 which equals- "Oh shit," I thought, "that's 90 miles an hour." I whispered to Bill, who was already real stoned, who replied laughing,"*Isn't that cool?*" Our now very stoned friends wanted to sober up and have some breakfast; it would be light in a couple of hours. They said that they would drive us to the border after breakfast and we could walk across the border back into the old USA. That sounded great to us having not eaten since lunch. We bought the cheapest stuff off the menu, which cost us about $6.00 of our money, leaving us with $19.00, and off we went to the old USA, our wonderful home land.

It was about 5:00am when we reached the border and, not suprisingly, were nervous about being let back into the country. We had been canoeing for a couple of weeks and been on the road now for about 10 hours and didn't look like the upstanding citizens that we were. Oh! We can't forget about all the partying that we had been doing , so it was not surprising that we got the dreaded " Please come with me boys." I had been through this routine, and had an idea what may be in store for us, remembering my experience with Andy, the last time I heard those dreaded words. *"Follow me boys"* That's right we got stripped searched again! Bill was a strip search virgin and it gave me a silent chuckle as I saw the look on his face. I thought now it is an even score; once by the Canoocks and once by the old USA. Border guards must like to strip smelly, grody guys. They went through are packs with a fine tooth comb, checked to see if we had any records, gave us the third degree and finally could find no more reasons to detain us and let us in. "*HOORAY BACK IN THE OLD USA*" we sang, as we walked away from the border.

It was now light and we didn't have to wait too long for our next ride. I guess this guy going to work in Duluth figured that we couldn't be too bad, since they had just let us into the country. He was a nice guy and we felt lucky to be driving with someone more sane, especially now that we were sober, and it wasn't long before we were in Duluth, where he dropped us off.

I had learned, on my first hitch hike adventure, that it is tough to get a ride in a city or town of any size, even though there is a ton of people, and was not surprised when no one was picking us up. It was 7:30 in the morning and people were just flying by, and of course we got a little hassle from a local cop who chilled after we recited our story to him, which we now had down pat. After about and an hour, we finally decided that our sign was not working so good, and wrote on the backside please help in big letters. We would flash the front side and then the backside, and began to think it may be a long walk back to Rockford, where the trash mobile was.

That's about the time our karma changed and we got our next ride all the way to Eau Claire, by a nice salesman who was really looking for some company. In my first hitch hike experiece, I had learned that traveling salesmen liked to pick hitch hikers up. It must be because they liked to talk. This guy fit right into the mold and talked our ears off. We didn't mind though, because our throats were sore from telling our story so many times and we were very thankful for the ride. He could have been a serial killer and we would have still taken our chances.

The salesman's destination was outside of Eau Claire and he let us out at the off ramp just out of town. We knew it was illegal to hitch hike on an expressway, but you could hitch hike before the on ramp, which we did. We were not looking forward to being hassled by any more cops and were lucky again and got another ride pretty quickly. This time it was a couple of guys heading back to school at the University of Wisconsin in Madison. Man were we lucky. We knew that Madison was only about two hours from Rockford and hoped to be home sometime that day.

In Madison, again after a command performance telling our story, we were let out at the off ramp and walked to the on ramp to hitch hike. Again, it wasn't long before we spotted this muscle car, racing up the on ramp, slamming on his breaks when he saw us. He was driving a muscle car, like all greasers drove in high school, and not much different from the guys in Canada.

A greaser, of course for those of you too young to remember, had wavy hair with a ton of hair gel, hence the name greaser, shiny pants and shirts and black shoes. These guys dressed like punk mob guys and hung out in gangs.. I was a dupper in high school, dressing in Farah pants, solid color like Dockers, madrass shirts, and penny loafers, but related to greassers also, because we got in so much trouble and liked to party and fight, which they could relate too. A muscle car is a car with a raised up suspention, souped up engine, loud muffler and usually a stick shift, that was really fast. Greasers' took great pride in these cars and loved to drive fast and race. A not uncommon practice was to race someone for the title of their car. In high school, the greaser girls had a reputation of being slutty and because of this we were always trying to get them to like us, but had no luck, because we were duppers. Oh to be in high school again. NOT!

We ran up to the car and asked him where he was going. He said, "Chicago" and we jumped in. He looked like a typical greaser, and was obviously upset. As he burned rubber he started to rant. "*F****** cops just gave me a ticket. That's my third one in a week,*" which he was in the process of ripping up and throwing out the window, as we were already doing 90. "Wow! Oh MY! Shit! Jeeze!" All these thoughts and more came to mind, but after the rides we had already had we were kinda used to traveling fast and being scared shitless and took it in stride.

It's amazing, traveling at 90, how fast we made it to Rockford. Of course, like always, we had been telling him our story, and Bill discovered that he didn't live too far from him in Chicago, and decided to take a chance, and take him up on the offer to go all the way to Chicago. They dropped me off at the Clock Tower Inn where the trash mobile was parked, Bill and I said our good byes and off they went.

As I dug my keys out of my pack, I thought, what an excellent adventure the hitch hike had turned out to be. I couldn't believe in had taken only 26 hours to get to my car. Life was good at the moment, and thought we may have even beat that F****** Tuck Well back. And fantasized about beating his brains to a pulp next time I saw him.

I thought how sad it was that things had changed since my first hitch hike in 1969, seven years before. The way things were trending, it wouldn't be long before nobody would hitch hike. People were getting a lot more paranoid it seemed, and I could certainly understand this. When we were young swamp rats, our parents did not have much concern about us being nabbed by some maniac. Things had changed now, with serial killers like Charlie Manson hitting the scene, and wondered why our country was producing people like the Manson Family. Little did I know then just how bad things would become, and how right my predictions were. Now, we have kids killing kids, kids killing adults, moms killing their kids, you get the idea, all the time. My experience is that most people are very nice and would like to help but fear rules their lives. Today you hardly ever see a hitch hiker.

We learned a lot on this adventure. First, when nobody would pick us up, try a sign. Second, if people seem untrustworthy, they probably are. Third, most people are nice. Fourth, travel is very fast when you get picked up by maniacs in souped up cars. Fifth, back seats are safer and always wear your seat belts. Last, but not the least, if you want to have great memories you have to have excellent adventures.

REALITY CHECK

Always after an excellent adventure there is a natural let down, when you go back to the reality of your life. My reality, at this point, was not too good. I was living in my old camper in a trailer park/campground that I knew couldn't go on much longer because it would soon be cold, making life in the GMC miserable. I had quit the band I had been playing with for the last several years, which had provided some good money. The canoe we are responsible hopefully made it to Pittsburg, and we will have to figure out a way to get it back. Sometimes reality sucks!

The first thing I did on Monday was to call Bill and check that everything on his end was good. He told me that the ride after I got out in Rockford was fine and said, *"I am planning to call Tuck soon."* I said *"Great tell him he's a Dick Wad for me."* Bill said *" I certainly will."* The next call I made was to Mike, my muiscian friend who I had been jamming with in Virgil, a small town of 150 people. He had some great news. He said, *" I found a place for you in Virgil. It's not the Ritz, but it's cheap."* I said, *"You know I have been living in my camper and before that I was living in the farm building with no running water. I don't need the Ritz."* He said, *"Great! You can come over anytime."* I said, *"How about now?"*

It didn't take me long to get to Virgil, which was only three miles from the campground that I was staying at. I went to Mike's house and we walked over to see my potential new home. It was on a large corner lot, maybe three or four acres, with an old large building behind it. The house was a forty feet wide and twenty feet deep ranch. It was a very basic building that looked like it had been converted into living quarters. I learned later that indeed it had. It was the local saloon for several years before it became my home, and heard several good stories of drucken escapades through the years from the locals. It had five rooms; a big bedroom and living room, small kitchen and crude bathroom with shower, and a small back room with water tank and pump. There was a small furnace in the bedroom. After what I had been living in for the last year, this was the Ritz. It was perfect for jamming with a band because there were no close neighbors. I'm sure this is exactly what Mike had in mind. The best part was the rent was only $150 dollars a month. And the landlords were a nice older couple who had converted the big old building, which used to be a milk processing plant, into a blacksmith shop on the bottom and an apartment on the top. Leonard, a nice large Sweed blacksmith and his wife Maybelle. And turned out to be great landlords and good friends. I asked them if I could make a few improvements and they said no problem as long as I asked them first. Little did I know that I was going to spend the next twevle years living there.

My reality was getting better by the minute, and they said that I could move in the first of September, which was in a few weeks. I called back Bill that evening and he told me that he had talked to Mr. Dick Wad Tuck.

He said, *"I yelled and screamed at him and tried to get some of our money back. Tuck said that we agreed to be responsible for the canoe and he wanted us to go get it. I told him to go F*** himself but it didn't help. He is a total dick and finally said OK and I got him* to give us half of our transportation money back." That was $90. I asked Bill why he stranded us in Canada. Tuck said," *By the time we walked up the rapids, and then*

walked out it was Tuesday evening and we couldn't wait a day for you" I said to Bill, "What an unbelievable Dick Wad. This guy couldn't wait one day. I think the real truth was that he didn't want to pay for the train tickets for the group." Bill said *"I agree. I know you are living in the GMC, and the trash mobile is getting old, so we could use the money to rent a car and take a weekend to drive up and back to Pittsburg"* I said, "Great another excellent adventure."

PITTSBURG

With both Bill's and mine teaching schedule in mind, we decided to go the next weekend. Bill rented a midsize car that got good gas milage. And planned to use the suction cup racks that I had to carry the boat back. I drove down to Bill's place early on Saturday and we left. What Bill didn't tell me, until we were already well on our way, was that he had rented the car for only one day. I said, "*What are you nuts!*" He said," *It is all that we could afford. We have to pay for the gas and food.*" We estimated that it would take us about 10 hours to get to Pittsburg. If we didn't spend much time there we might be able to make it, but it would be close.

We only stopped for gas and fast food and switched drivers every tank of gas. We made good time and found Jack's place at about the ten and a half hour mark. It was great to see Jack again and he told us of his ordeal to get the van fixed, which took about eight days, because the mechanic had to wait for Volkswagon parts. He said the van ran flawlessly on the ride home and he had no problems. We told him about our hitch hike home and what a dick wad Tuck was. He showed us this cool survival hand gun that had two barrels and shot 45 caliber hand gun loads and 410 shot gun shells. He offered to put us up for the night. We thanked him and said we had to get the car back by 8:00 tomorrow morning.

He said, "*What are you nuts?*" I said, "*No not nuts, just young and stupid,*" and off we went, sadly never to see or talk to him again. I often wonder how Jack is doing and wished we had kept in touch. "*Hey Jack if you read this book. Give me a call.*"

We blew about an hour at Jacks talking and getting the boat tied on the car, and left at 7:30pm. We knew we had to book, so we stretched the speed limit and rock and rolled. On the way out we had a great half hour machine going trashing Tuck and talking about the trip, and continued in this vane, until the wee hours of the late night when Billy caught some Z's, which made for an anti half hour machine. Time seemed to stand still. Most people have experienced late night tired driving. This is the most dangerous time to be behind the wheel, and the most not fun. Over the road truckers can only drive so much in every 24 hours, because of this danger. I have even heard, in states like Montana, where there are generous speed limits, they will give you a ticket for driving fast at night, because of the danger.

I was trying hard not to fall asleep when suddenly I thought, "*what the heck was that?*" It looked like a large elephant.*" No this was not from partying, which we smartly weren't doing. I quickly figured out that I was hallucinating. "*Holy shit,*" I thought. I am really burned out and quickly woke up Billy, told him that I was so tired that I was halucinating and we switched. We both struggled to stay awake to finish our marathon drive. At this point, we both knew what a dumb ass plan this was and I said to Billy "*This was a dumb ass plan.*" We learned that day if you start seeing weird stuff while driving, it's time to stop. We made it back, thank God alive, just in time to switch the canoe on to the trash mobile and return the rental car. I crashed at Bill's place for about six hours and headed for home.

Bill made plans to return the canoe to Tuck the next weekend. I picked Bill up at the train station which was fairly close Saturday morning. We met Tuck at the Clock Tower Inn again in Rockford that afternoon. I guessed, he smartly didn't want us to know where he lived, and was worried about confronting us!

I had already called Ben and had heard the story and knew that Ben was serious about giving Tuck some serious grief that he deserved. Also, I just happened to run into a good friend of mine, Butch Polan, while at a watering hole that the band had played a lot, and I sometimes hung out at. Well, maybe hung there way too much. Butch was the director of an outdoor program in Rockford, for troubled kids. We were shooting the shit about my recent trip, and of course Tuck Well's name came up. He said, *"That's interesting, Tuck has just applied for a job with me."* "Boy, you gotta believe in Karma," I exclaimed. Butchy had already gotten the idea of what bad news Tuck was. He said,*"Man I'm glad I ran into you. I was really thinking of hiring him, but now-NO WAY!"* He continued, *"This guy really can sling a good line of shit. According to him he is an outdoor superstar."* I said, "He is a dick wad supper star. He couldn't find his way out of a paper bag." Butchy said,*"Man I can't believe that he did that to you. What a dick wad. "* "Yippy," I thought! "Now I don't have to pound his face in and probably go to jail, which would definitely wreck my day, and Tuck is not worth that. It's just what that dick wad deserves." This knowledge had a calming effect on me, and now I felt ready to confront Tuck, without going postal on him.

When we arrived at the Clock Tower Inn of course, you guessed it. Tuck wasn't there and we had to wait. Gee, what a surprise! He showed up with Jan, his girl friend, and Mike the helper guide. Again, this proved my theory about Tuck being nervous and he knew, in his soul, what a dick wad he was. Both Jan and Mike were very nice and it was great to see them. I remember fondly sharing Mike's tent when Billy was struck by the camp plague, and Jan was always very helpful around camp. I often wondered how

Tuck brainwashed this girl into liking him. Although, he did have a good line of crap like Butchy said.

It was an awkward situation to say the least, because Tuck probably thought I was going to put a hurt on him. Little did he know that I had talked to Butchy and was going to enjoy putting another kind of hurt on him.

Bill and I were both mellow and we calmly took the canoe off my car and put it on Tuck's van. We got it tied down and I calmly said to Tuck, "*Hey, Butchy Polan's, a good friend of mine. He told me you applied for a job from him. Good luck with that.*" The look on his face was priceless, as Bill and I walked away never to see him again!

NEW CANOE AND GEAR

The good thing about living in shacks is it is cheap. In fact, when I was living in the farm out-building it did not cost any money, except for investing about $300 dollars making it livable. I lived there for a year and saved lots of money. I have followed this philosophy for my entire life, which has given me the means to follow my dreams. No, not living in shacks, but to always-live way cheaper than what you make. My current dream was to get some new gear and canoe, which I had the bucks to buy.

When I met George Steed on the Wolf River, where we beat the crap out of Mike's, my musician friend's canoe, he showed me how his canoe was rigged. He talked about the new material, Royalex, manufactured by Uniroyal, which his canoe was made from. It consisted of an outer layer of vinyl, layers of ABS plastic, a center of foam and then ABS and vinyl again. The canoe is made by heating sheets of Royalex in an oven then placing it over a form, which in a few minutes becomes a canoe. Because of this, the boat remembers its shape. The material is relatively light and tough as hell, all of which makes it the best choice for running whitewater and wilderness tripping. I wanted one! I began to shop.

At this time, I determined that there were three canoes which suited my needs. A 16-foot Mad River Explorer, a 17-foot Blue Hole and a 17-foot 2-inch Old Town Tripper. I had already checked out the Mad River and the Blue Hole, and really wanted to see the Old Town. When I was talking to Leonard, my landlord, which we did a lot because we both loved to talk, I happened to mention the Chicagoland Canoe Base and its owner Ralph Freese. Leonard said that Ralph was a blacksmith and he knew him well and offered to call him and see if he could get me a deal. He did just that, and I made plans to go to Chicago. I picked up Bill, and we trucked right over to Ralph's canoe shop.

Ralph was a real character. He looked like a fur trader and seemed put out just to talk to us, which was odd because we were customers, until I told him who I was. He said *"Hey you're the youngster that Leonard told me about who is looking for a canoe."* I said, *"Yeah, I've been looking for a good tripping canoe."* He said, *"I just re-enacted the Rene'-Robert Cavalier expedition from Montreal to the Gulf of Mexico and know a thing or two about tripping."* I said, *"Cool."* His eyebrows went up. I said I was interested in the Old Town tripper. He said, *"It ain't birch bark, but it has a good design and is really tough, being made out of Royalex."*

It was love at first sight, and to boot he gave me a great deal. The Tripper is a seventeen-foot two-inch canoe with about three inches of rocker, and a twenty-five-inch bow height. It has very good primary stability and nice rounded sides, giving it great secondary stability. Primary stability is how stable the boats feels when you first get in, and are just sitting there. Secondary stability is the ability of the canoe to heal over, without tipping over. The Tripper's flat bottom gives the boat its good stable primary stability. The downside of a flat bottom is that it does not move the best through the water so it is no speed demon, but plenty fast for my needs. Rocker is the upward sweep of the ends of the canoe.

Imagine the tripper on a flat surface; the ends would be 3 inches above the ground. The rocker in a boat lifts the ends out of the water making it turn easier. When the ends of a canoe are deep in the water it helps the boat track straight and not turn.

When the tripper has a load, the ends will sink allowing the boat to track straight. The Tripper has a lot of volume or displacement, how much water a boat displaces (volume). This determines how much it can haul. The Tripper, on the many thousand of miles of excellent adventures, has never let me down.

Ralph gave a good deal on foam flotation blocks that went into the stern and the bow, which helps the boat float better in a tip over, making it easier to control when upside down. A big boat like this holds about 200 gallons of water. Water weighs about 8 pounds a gallon. That is a whopping 1600 pounds flying down the river when full of water. Being caught between it and a rock or tree is not a good plan. Maybe this is where the saying, never get caught between a rock and a hard place comes from. A good plan is to turtle the boat, which then becomes a breeze to control, floating high because of the flotation in the ends, making the canoe hugely safer. I also bought some D-rings and webbing, to make thigh straps, as Jack showed us how to do. The thigh straps connect the paddler to the boat giving the canoe lots of stability. This is very useful when being hit by big waves. In other words, it is a great swim preventer!

As you know, through the school of hard knocks, I learned how important the right gear is on a wilderness canoe trip. Remember, how I pinned a canoe on the Wolf River, and we were damn lucky not to pin a canoe on the Missinaibi trip. Pinning a canoe is when the canoe fills up with water and then goes against an obstacle, like a rock or a tree, and bends it like a tin can or rips in half. You can see how this may not make your day. The above-mentioned flotation also helps prevent this nightmare from happening. You might be interested to know that today we use float bags and not foam. Back in 1976 foam was the only option. Royalex has the best chance of surviving a pin, especially if it has floatation. Through the years, I have been involved in many pinning situations and have never lost a boat yet. And have gained a few which others could not get unpinned!

The proper clothing is very important for a safe and comfortable trip. It was not a good feeling to see my rain pants ripped off while walking a rapid on the second day of the Missinaibi trip. *"Not good,"* I thought then! *"I should have spent a few extra bucks on a better raincoat and pants."* Although, I did discover on the trip, that rain pants were not necessary. If you keep your trunk and head dry and warm, your whole body will be warm. Fast drying pants are the ticket. Pants with a high amount of nylon or all nylon will dry fast and keep you warm. They are also very tough. Stay away from cotton! When it gets wet, it stays wet and you freeze. Water takes body heat away very fast! You would be better off stark naked than having wet cotton on your body. Shoes are also very important. They protect your feet from sharp stuff on the bottom of the river. Remember George, who cut the heck out of his foot.

Back in 1976 there were not a lot of choices for footgear. High top canvas boots or gym shoes were the best choices back then, but today there is a great assortment of quality footgear. Many times, we have had customers come into our outfitting shop because they lost their shoes in the river. I test people's footgear, by trying to pull them off their feet, when they come for a class or trip. If I cannot, then the river may not either. Another danger on the river is foot entrapment, getting your foot caught between rocks, logs, or whatever may be lurking in the depths. If you get your feet caught and there is a good current, you can be pushed over and then under the water. This can cause you to drown, even if you have a life jacket on! You can see why sleek footwear is an important consideration when choosing footwear. I use neoprene booties designed specifically for paddlers. They are tough, warm, sleek, and offer good traction on wet rocks, and will stay on your feet even when walking in the worse black river muck.

In the Boundary Waters, a canoe area that borders Northern Minnesota and Canada, there are many sharp granite rocks on well-worn portage trails, which can be very tough on neoprene booties and your feet. I decided to look for tougher options in footgear on a planned trip there. I discovered boots designed for fly fisherman, for wading rivers. They were high top, which would make them stay on my feet, tough and had felt soles for good traction on wet rocks. I thought, *"Great these should be a good alternate to my neoprene boots on those nasty portage trails, and I can wear some neoprene socks inside for warmth."* I dumbly did not consider how bulky they were. Big mistake! I have never been a big fan of portaging, I use every other alternative possible, like paddling up the rapid, lining the canoe, or even walking up a rapid. I was paddling with Neal, a client from Chicago, on a ninety-mile trip in the Boundary Waters. And decided walking up a rapid was our best option, when, to my shock, the bottom was covered with these very big irregular sharp rocks, and I got my foot caught. We were in two-foot waves and I was scared shitless. I screamed at my partner Neal, *"My foot is stuck hold the boat stable."* "OK," he shouted back. I was stable and screamed back to him. *"Move the boat just a little back."* That did the trick and my foot came unstuck, but man was that scary, something I do not ever want to repeat. I had my regular neoprene boots with as a back up, and needless to say, that was the last time I wore those bulky boots, which went into the trash as soon as the trip was over.

Another piece of gear that is very important to bring is a rain tarp or simple rain shelter. On the trip with Neal in the Boundary

Waters, it poured for 6 days straight. It rained so much that after the trip was over, we had a hard time getting out, because of some washed out roads. You are probably thinking that the trip had to be horrible, with all that rain. To the contrary, it was great. We both had the proper clothing to stay warm and I had bought this cool lean-to shelter, that I had just bought, for just such occasions. It was simple to set up, had no-see-um netting, and afforded us a dry and bug free place to cook and hang out. It packed up small and only weighed a couple of pounds.

And the other benefit, from all that rain, is we did not have to portage much, because of the high water. This particular trip started on Hog Creek and traveled through several rivers and lakes, with a whopping 55 portages. We did only ten, having a blast paddling thru all the rapids, instead of walking the portages. Rain can be a great thing as long as you have the right gear!

When shopping for my canoe I discovered Thermarest mattresses in a paddling shop. Up to this point, we had used solid foam ground pads, which were not very comfortable, especially when sleeping on hard rock or stones. I spied these ground pads that I had never seen and asked the owner of the shop, *"What's the deal with this new ground pad?"* He replied, *"These are the coolest things since sliced bread."* He then threw a bunch of stuff (tent stakes, pens, etc.) on the floor, put the Thermarest pad on top and told me to lie on the pad. I could not believe it; I did not feel a thing. I said, *"Cool, I'll take one!"* These pads are a combination of foam and air. They self-inflate to almost full, needing only a few puffs of air to finish the job. No way, would I go on a canoe trip without my Thermarest pad.

I also bought a new tent that day. It was a mountaineering tent, capable of withstanding

100-mile winds. Before on a three-day canoe trip, on the Flambeau River in Wisconsin, we got hit with very high straight-line winds, which bent the heck out of the aluminum poles of our tent. We were able to bend the poles back, but something a little tougher, lighter and smaller, I thought, would be a good idea.

From bad experiences caused by being overloaded, I learned how important it is to pack light and small. Everything must fit into your pack and boat, which should never be overloaded. The manufacturers of canoes and kayaks often list the maximum load for their boats. I found through the years that this commonly exceeds, by a lot, what I would recommend for the proper safe weight in a canoe, kayak or any boat. The rounded sides of a boat are what gives its seaworthiness, the ability to handle waves without tipping over. If those rounded sides are under the water, there is nothing to support the sides when the boat heals and you go over. The heavier your packs and gear are the greater chance you have of hurting yourself. If you hurt your back or anything else, while lifting monstrous packs, you can become totally incapacitated. This is not a good situation in the wilderness. You know what I mean if you have ever struggled over a portage trail. There are no stores on a wilderness trip, to replace broken gear, or doctor's offices, to repair broken bodies.

The philosophy of going light begins with the premise that you can always make do, as long as you have the basic needs for comfort and survival. What are these basic needs? First, you have to have clean water and food. The water part is easy as long as you can filter and treat the water, because you are by water. There are excellent lightweight water treatment systems on the market today. The basic method we used back in 1976 was adding iodine or bleach to the water, making sure the water boiled when cooking and being careful not to use any water around where there was any sign of beaver or moose. There is a parasite that can be in water even when it looks perfectly clear that comes from beaver and moose poop. Packing lightweight food that is nutritious, tasty, won't spoil and is easy to prepare is a challenge and takes skill and careful planning. Today there are some excellent companies that specialize in lightweight food. And making your own jerky and dried fruit and vegetables is fun, saves you money, and is a very good option. Always pack a couple of extra days of food, which you should never eat until you are off the river unless you love to starve and chant *"Cheeseburgers, Cheeseburgers."*

Second, you need shelter from the elements. You get this from a good quality, lightweight, no more than four pounds per person, tent. Then add a light rain fly to cook in the rain. Tents must be waterproof, even in the worst down pour, bug proof, and tough. Look for a tent with a good full coverage rain fly, no- see-um netting (very fine netting found on all good quality tents), light aluminum poles, and at least number seven zippers. Zipper failure is very common in inexpensive tents. Tuck did teach, everyone of us who went on his warm up weekend trip, how awful it is to be hassled by mosquitos all night as we slept under the stars.

Third, you need a good sleeping bag. The temperature in the northern wilderness can vary wildly. I had an inexpensive down sleeping bag, rated to 40 degrees, and I was cold some nights on the Missinaibi River trip. It is not fun to be cold! Down is the warmest and lightest of all materials, even today with the many synthetic materials on the market. And back in 1977 the options were limited. It was hard to find a good down bag let alone a good synthetic bag back then. The big downfall of down is that it loses most of its insulation value when wet. If you get your down bag wet, it is a useless wet lump. I have another great story about just this, I will it save for a later book.

Sleeping bags tend to be rated lower than their real comfort range. A good rule of thumb is to add 20 degrees, to the rating and when you get below freezing it is wise to add even a little more. I found a great bag to replace my old cold one, that was rated to -25 degrees; I do not like to be cold. It was constructed out of quality down, making it small enough to fit into my waterproof bag, and not too heavy. The only problem was, it was available only in kit form. That is how hard good gear was to find in 1977. Remember my friends, Chris and Deanne, who I had lived with for several years. Deanne loved to sew and agreed, for a little compensation, to sew the kit for me.

Fourth, you need an insulating ground pad to sleep on. If you sleep directly on the ground or on an air mattress without insulation, you will freeze. The cold ground or air underneath you will suck all the heat out of you. A type of ground pad that combines insulating qualities with comfort, and is light and small is the best choice.

Fifth, you will need the proper clothing as I described before and a quality rain gear. You will only need one set of clothes with a back up set, in case something is destroyed. And packed away in your waterproof bag.

Sixth, you need a compact cook kit, which includes a very light and small stove, just enough cook gear to cook what you need and no more. And it is a good idea to also pack a small and very light grate that you can use in case something happens to your stove or you run out of fuel. We left our cook kit once on a 500-mile trip and survived quite nicely cooking over a fire.

Seventh, you need good maps, a couple of compasses (one in your life jacket and one in your waterproof bag), a light weight saw, a small flashlight or headlamp, a bottle for water, a small but complete medical kit, and a knife on your life jacket.

Once you have the basic and most important items you can, if you are light enough, add some fluff. Believe me, if you have the above basic needs met, you will be a happy camper. If you are cold, wet, eaten by mosquitoes or scared shitless all the time because your boat is overloaded and dread portaging, you will not be having fun. On the other hand, if it takes you 15 minutes to set up camp, cooking is a breeze, meals are easy, filling, and delicious, and you have only a few pots to clean, life becomes very sweet. Waterproof bags, tents, flotation bags, helmets, canoes, paddles, life jackets etc. have continued to improve making your excellent adventures today even better.

"Here is a quick note." At the time of writing this book, Ralph Freese died at age 85. He followed his dreams and made a great contribution to canoeing, conservation, and educating our younger generation. He will be remembered fondly.

TRIP PLANNING

Even, or in spite of Tuck Well, the trip on the Missinaibi River was enjoyable and a great success. I must give him credit for giving me two things. One, was a lesson in how not to plan and guide a trip. Two, was a desire to plan and guide an extended trip on my own. When we departed from our group and we were on our own, the trip was fabulous. Tuck did not have the knowledge to guide a trip like this. If he did, he would have realized that he, nor the group, did not have the paddling skills or experience to do this trip. He also should have realized what a difference water levels could make on the nature of a river. In our case, the water was low, not unexpected in August, which made for a lot of walking our canoes. On the other hand, if the water had been high, the rapids on the Missinaibi may have wrecked some boats or possibly killed someone. I learned a lot, as you know already, from screwing up on my own, which is how we hopefully get wisdom. I discovered early, that I really enjoyed planning trips. No, not screwing up, planning a trip, and felt confident that now I was ready. So here we go! The next year I started planning for my very own extended wilderness trip.

The first part in planning a trip is to decide where to go. I decided to stick with Ontario Canada, because it was reasonably close and

I had already traveled there three times. This made me somewhat familiar with the province. Next, I started researching all the possible river trips in Ontario. Back in 1976, there was no internet, which made finding information a lot harder. I had picked up a book "Canoe Routes in Ontario", which had lots of contact information including contact information for the Ministry of Natural Resources. I wrote them, and they sent me a packet of information on 125 canoe routes in Ontario. *"Great!"* I thought.

I spent several weeks perusing the short descriptions of these trips. I finally settled on the Allenwater River. They described the Allenwater as a 14-day trip, 130 miles in length, with short well-cleared portages, twenty-foot waterfalls, areas of whitewater, and good fishing. The cool thing about this trip was that it was similar to the Missinaibi River trip, because there was a train that we could use for the shuttle. The only difference was the train ride came first, with the trip ending only a couple of miles away from where we would leave our vehicle in the train parking lot. One of the hardest things about doing a canoe trip is the shuttle. You can pay someone to help like an outfitter, or you can hike, bike, motorcycle, walk or take two cars.

To this day, I cannot figure out why Tuck didn't utilize the second car we had on our trip to do the shuttle. He simply could have driven his rig back to Cochrane, followed by our second car, which then would have brought him back to the start. I think the problem was, we were behind schedule and he did not want to take the extra time. Although, this could have been done while everyone was packing the food. Well, enough about Tuck.

Ok, now I need some maps and people to go with me. I gave Bill a call and he said, *"Hell yes, sounds like a blast."* Then I talked to Chris and his wife Deanne, who I had lived with and saw often, and they were interested. Chris said, *"Deanne's parents own a*

Montgomery Ward canoe, which I think we could borrow. I think it is made out of fiberglass." I said, "*Fiberglass is not the best, but it might be OK, as long as it has a decent hull design.*" I have my crew now, but still need more information.

I had already written to the Canadian Map Office, which was part of the Department of Energy Mines and Resources, and they sent me three map indexes of Canada where I could order topographical maps. I spent several days figuring out just what maps I needed and what scale. I got a 1:250,000 map, which would give me a good overview of the whole trip, and a bunch of 1:50,000 maps, which would give me more detail, and be better for navigation.

The Allenwater River was a typical drop and pool Canadian Shield River where the river would flow into a lake, then a series of rapids or falls into a river, and back into a lake and so forth. This would mean that it would take careful orienteering to navigate several of the large lakes. Jack had taught Bill and I the basics of orienteering. You take a bearing from the map, and then sight that bearing on a point in the distance and travel there. It seemed easy but I knew it would be a challenge for a beginner, which I was. I knew what it was like to be lost, been there done that, and I did not want to make an encore performance of that.

I began to review in my mind, all the things that I had learned by screwing up, when my paddling days had begun at age twelve. I learned that paddling skills were very important, so I would have to work with Chris and Deanne to build their skills so they would be able to handle the whitewater we would encounter on the trip. Bill and I had both learned from Jack on the Missinaibi, so that was cool, but we needed some quality time to get used to my new canoe. As you know I had been upgrading a lot of my own paddling gear and would have to make sure we all had sufficient gear, which was also light. I knew how dangerous an overloaded boat was and how portaging a big load is a nightmare. Chris and Deanne lived close by and we had a local river to paddle, so this should be no problem, I thought. I learned how important the right food was, and would not include any fresh food that could make us sick. This would be the biggest challenge of our trip, I contemplated. I knew my canoe was designed and rigged for trips just like this, and knew we would have to put some flotation and straps in Chris and Deanne's canoe to make it much safer. And I would have to get a good lightweight cook set and stove together. I was planning to take the GMC camper, but had no way of hauling the boats on top of the camper. WEW! My head was spinning with all the things that needed to get done.

The next weekend I got together with Chris and Deanne for a little fun and soon found out that they were really into the trip and spent the night partying and planning. I thought *"How great, all this work was going to be fun with the help of Chris and Deanne."* We spent many weekends through the winter doing just that. We found a good recipe for beef jerky that we could make it the oven, and found a source for some freeze-dried food. I ordered a Colman Peak I stove; a single burner light backpack stove, that burned Colman fuel and a container to put it in which should work great for canoeing. Andy and I had driven through Ely Minnesota, one of the gateways to the Boundary Waters, on the way back from our first trip to Canada. The Boundary Waters is a canoe area that borders Northern Minnesota and Canada. In one of their many canoe shops, we found a cool thing called a Tote Oven. It consisted of two pieces of heavy aluminum, shaped like pots, with a fire ring on the bottom of one of them. They fit together making an oven, and they did not weigh a lot. It came with two handles, making two pots, which could be put together making it a great Dutch oven or used as pots. I realized that our bowls, cups, and utensils could fit inside of the oven making a great light cook kit.

The aluminum container I had ordered with the backpack stove could also double as two smaller pots giving us four pots, making a great light and tough compact cook kit. We talked about quick drying, clothes, raincoats, sleeping bags, hats, waterproof bags, shoes and tents, and by spring we were all ready to go, and dying to get some practice in on the river.

MERAMEC RIVER MISSOURI

Bill called me up one day in early spring and said, *"Rich, our college buddy who lived in Quincy, wondered if we would be interested in paddling the Meramec in Missouri. Rich said he and some of his friends paddle the Meramec every couple of years and wondered if we wanted to meet them down there."* I told Bill," *That sounds great and it would be a perfect trial run for our trip!"* It would give us the opportunity to work with Chris and Deanne on their paddling skills and to get comfortable with each other. I had not seen Rich since our adventure in the cave and flash flood, before, sadly, our other college friend Billy, had died in the fire in Mellen, and knew it would be a great party to boot. I called up Chris and Deanne and they said it sounded great.

We had one big problem. I still did not have a way to carry two canoes on top of the GMC. Then it came to me. DUH! Leonard, my landlord, could probably make me one. The next day I went over to his shop, and talked to him. He said, *"I'm not too busy now, so I get can to work right away if you can help."* I said, *"Sure."* It is quite cool to see a blacksmith at work. First, we talked about what I wanted. I said, *"I need something very stable and strong so*

I can put at least two canoes on top of the camper with no worries about wind." He then checked out the camper, took a bunch of measurements, talked to himself for a while, and then ambled over to a giant area where he had all manner of steel. Soon he was cutting, bending, and welding, and I was gophering. It wasn't long before Leonard had fabricated a very cool and extremely strong rack and the problem was solved. He then said, *"You have been very nice in helping me out with other things so all I need is a little money for the materials."* I said, *"Thanks!"*

Chris, Deanne and I packed up a bunch of food, and of course a little bit of spirits, or maybe a lot of spirits. I knew how Rich liked to party and had no doubts that his friends would not be any different, and threw in a giant bottle of aspirin too. We got my new canoe and their Montgomery Ward canoe on the brand-new rack on top of camper. For those youngsters out there, you properly have never heard of Montgomery Wards, which was like a Sears department store or Target. Their boat was made out of fiberglass, not light but surprisingly had a good design that was well suited to canoe tripping. We did not even need a ¼ mile of rope to tie the canoes. It was just too easy with this new rack. One person stood on the hood of the truck, you could not do that on today's trucks, while the other person pushed the boat until the hood person got a hold of it. With a couple of bungee cords, we were good to go. Chris, who was the pusher because he was taller, was able to stand on the large back bumper in back to hook bungee cords. The camper was a full camper that you could stand up in with a bed over the cab. Leonard's talking to himself, really paid off. It was perfect. Now I really understood the difference between a welder and a blacksmith. A blacksmith designs and fabricates cool stuff from scratch like this incredible canoe rack.

We picked up Bill at the train station the night before we left. He crashed with me and we left early the next morning. As you already know, traveling in the GMC isn't fast, it only cruises about 60mph, but it is a great way to travel. We were meeting Rich and friends at a campground near Rolla, off highway 44 in Missouri, and figured it would only take us about seven hours to get there. Nine hours later, after an uneventful trip, we arrived.

It was early evening and we found Rich and friends, already partying hardy. I think the statute of limitations has expired, so maybe we had a few already too. Rich showed us what not to put in a fire. Poison Ivy vines! He said if you burn the vines and breathe in the smoke, you could get poison ivy all over your body. Yikes! Andy, who you remember got blown into the forest and into a poison ivy patch, has struggled with reactions to poison ivy ever since. It seems that most people have a natural immunity until you get a bad exposure, like Andy had. Since that time, when he got it bad, he would get it again every time we went canoeing and I would never get it. I did not know how lucky I was then and should have paid more attention to Rich. When you get down south, there is poison ivy everywhere and you really have to learn to avoid it. Isn't hindsight great! There will be more on this subject latter.

The next day we all got up with mild hangovers, yeah right, good thing we had plenty of aspirin, but fun was had by all. It is now time to hit the river. One of the great things about meeting friends to paddle is that you have a way to shuttle. The Meramec River is a popular river with many outfitters around to do shuttles, unfortunately, that is not the case with many great rivers that you may want to paddle. Through the years, we have used bicycles, and motorcycles. It is relatively easy to transport a bicycle but not so much for a motorcycle. The following year I purchased a 250cc Suzuki dirt-street bike and we put it on a rack on the front bumper of the GMC. The bike weighted about 300 pounds, so you could only do this with a heavy-duty truck. The rack was designed for the rear bumper, but we wouldn't be unable to get in the camper if it was on the back, so we put it on the front, which worked ok, except it did impede the headlights a little. Who needs to see anyway?

When my wife, Marcia, came on the scene, we used her T-top Chevy Camaro as a canoe car. We installed a hitch on the back, and then we purchased a motorcycle carrier that went on the hitch. The front wheel of the bike went into a cradle with a couple tie downs to the bike. The only problem was the bike would fall down unless you took the corners fast. No down side there, we got good at zooming around corners! You should now be thinking, how the heck did we transport the canoe, and the rest of our gear in this small car? Well, we took the back seat out and put a large Duluth pack on top of the T-tops. We then put the canoe over it, making it a car top carrier, with some foam blocks on gunwales, and tied her down.

On one trip to Florida, where we planned to canoe and scuba dive, we had the car so overloaded that we broke a rear spring. And replaced these springs with a couple of real heavy-duty ones. And the car now, could handle the load and when empty it had a great rear end muscle car look, although the ride was a little truck like. We routinely put heavier springs on all our vehicles, so much so that we became good friends with the people at the spring shop. We did several trips to Florida and Canada with this set up, with little problems, except for all the people staring at us with their mouths wide open. You can now see why Marcia was the perfect wife for me; she didn't even mind all the stares we would get from other people, or the abuse of her baby blue Camaro. And I am sure she never envisioned her beautiful Camaro, with a canoe on top and a motorcycle on the back.

Bill drove the GMC for the shuttle and I began to work with Chris and Deanne on their paddling skills. As you remember, I followed the technique that Jack had taught Bill and I and started by teaching the draw and push away strokes, which are designed to move the boat sideways without turning it. This is very helpful in a current because when the boat starts to turn sideways the current will catch the canoe and move it where you may not want to go. Next, I taught them the sweep and reverse sweep, which are turning strokes. I then explained how to ferry a canoe. Ferrying a canoe is the technique that uses the current to move the boat sideways. Using this technique enables you to stop your canoe in fast water by back paddling, then pitching it just right and the canoe will move sideways to where you want to be. I explained how useful this would be if you were heading toward a rock or strainer, or if a tree is down in the river and you really do not want to smash into it. You simply back paddle, pitch the boat so the current catches you on one side, back paddle again and this will move the boat in the opposite direction away from the obstacle. I told them that we would work on this and eddy turns when we got into the river. An eddy develops behind anything that blocks the current, including shorelines, rocks, or trees. Eddies have many uses including, places to get out of the current, reading rapids and they offer a safe protected way to get off the river. By this time Bill, Rich and friends were back and it was time to paddle. It was a beautiful spring day and we were all excited to get on the river.

The Meramec is a beautiful clear spring fed river, with fast current and easy rapids and was a perfect practice run for our trip. Chris and Deanne worked hard. They realized how they would soon need these skills, and fun was had by all.

Remember our caving adventure down in Quincy, when we were trapped by the flash flood? Well, Rich said, *"The outfitter over yonder,"* he was into speaking southern, *"told me about a cool cave we could explore, just over by that holler and up."* Bill and I, remembering our last experience in a cave said together. *"I don't* *know."* Rich said, "Common you P*****." We replied, *"Ok, but we need a few brews first."* Bill, Rich, Chris and I, armed with lights, lantern, rope, and a snoot full of liquid courage, took off in a quest to find the cave.

It took us awhile but we found a small hole way up on the top of a bluff that went straight down. Rich exclaimed, *"This must be it. The outfitter said it was a small opening that opens up into a large room."* I said, *"Man, its straight down."* Chris was the tallest of us all. He said," *We got rope and I'll go first."* He did. We tied the rope to Chris and he entered the hole. He yelled back, *"It's not bad at all. Oh shit, its straight down,"* He exclaimed, as he slid down the hill. *"I'm ok now just hold on to the rope tight. It's bad for a few feet but then there is a more gradual path down,"* he shouted. We tied the rope to a tree and all of us entered the cave. I thought, *"Yeah right"* as the path was much steeper than Chris had explained. *"Good thing I had a snoot full or I wouldn't be in this damn cave,"* I thought. It was a little way down to another small opening, where we all squeezed through on our bellies, into a spectacular large chamber. We all said, *"Wow!"* There were tons of stalactites and stalagmites, don't ask me which is which, because I can never remember. One hangs down from the ceiling and one goes up from the floor.

We worked our way down a couple more levels, to a dead end. Then Bill exclaimed, *"Let's get out here I need a brew."* We were all on the same page and heartedly agreed. We turned around and "uh oh." Chris asked, *"Which way?"* The last time we were in a cave, we had the common sense to run a string behind us so we could follow it back out of the cave, but this time, in our not so clear state, we forgot the string. Maybe the brews had something to do with this? After a short group panic and another hour of wallowing in the mud, we finally found the way back to the grand room.

Now we have to deal with," *the not too bad steep path*" to get out. We were all very tired at this point and were barely able to pull ourselves out. When we accomplished this we all gave a cheer *"Hooray, we're out,"* or more accurately *"We are finally out of that f***** cave.* Luckily, we could see the campground from the top of the bluff and after knee whacking and falling, because our lights were about dead, we finally made it back to camp.

You go into a cave nice and clean and you come out a mud pie. It was funny when we got back, maybe not for Chris; Deanne read him the riot act. She said, *"What happened, I was worried sick. You have been in the damn cave for three hours and you look like a mud pie."* Chris said," We *got a little lost can you get me a brew?"* She said," Get *your own damn brew and throw your mud pie ass into the river."* We all laughed and did just that.

Chris was soon forgiven and we spent the rest of the night partying hard. We hit the road after saying our goodbyes to Rich and our new friends the next morning. We had an uneventful trip, except for our hangovers. We passed the time planning a paddle on the Kishwaukee River, a local river close to where we lived. We talked about all the aspects of our upcoming trip, which made a perfect half hour machine and what an excellent adventure the weekend had provided.

NOW WHAT?

Just before we were ready to go on our last shake down paddle, Chris called and said, *"We have a problem!"* *"Uh Oh!"* I thought. He said, *"Deanne and I are parting ways."* *"Wow,"* I thought! This was shocking news and I asked him, *"What happened?"* He said, *"We have irreconcilable differences about the future."* That put a real damper on our plans and my mood suddenly crashed. I never saw this coming. I had lived with Chris and Deanne for many years, liked them both, and never dreamed this would ever happen. But, it did.

After a couple of weeks of trying to find someone for the trip Chris called out of the blue and said he had met a girl Ellen, who wanted to go. *"Well, all righty,"* I thought! The trip is back on. Then I thought this was a little too Tuck like. And I was very concerned about her lack of preparation for a Canadian Wilderness trip. I told Chris we would have to make sure that she was ready for the trip and scheduled a Kishwaukee trip to give Ellen a crash course in paddling a canoe. Ellen did very well, my concerns eased, and Chris assured me that he would bring her up to speed with her clothes and other gear and they would be ready. I trusted his judgment and said, *"Sounds Good*!"

Chris and I finished packing all the food and gear, loaded up the GMC, picked Bill up at the train station and waited for Ellen to arrive. Ellen arrived timely. We went to leave and RATS! Doorknob on the camper will not work! We cannot get in. This is not a good way to start a trip, and again I thought of Tuck. We messed with it and it seemed to work, but we did not get on the road until 11:00pm. I bet Ellen was wondering *"what the heck she got herself into."* Do these words sound familiar to you? *"Eh gads, am I as bad as Tuck; Nah, just a little wrinkle in the plan,"* I thought.

The GMC was running great and travel went well. Of course, with two teams to drive, the GMC was like a train. We only stopped for food, liquor, gas and to take care of nature's call. We made good time and the non-drivers were able to sleep, party, or whatever in the back. Things went well until, at the first gas and pit stop, the door acted up again and we had another delay and a big surprise. Ellen confessed to forgetting her money. *"Oh no,"* I thought. They may not let us into Canada if we do not have enough money. We declared all our food at the border, paid our tariff and got really nervous when the border officer asked how much money we had. Man, it was a good thing Chris had an extra stash of cash on him. They let us in. That was close! Again, too much like Tuck I thought, *"Maybe this trip planning is harder than I thought."*

We arrived in Armstrong, after a stop in Thunder Bay to find supplies, well, maybe for a lot of beer. This is not an easy task in Canada because beer and spirits are only sold at government stores, which are not plentiful. Being an important quest to our young partying souls, of course, we were successful eventually and off we went to find the 160 mile gravel road north of Thunder Bay to Armstrong, where we would end and start our trip. It was not hard to find, because there are not lots of roads traveling north in Canada. We were all anxious to get there and it seemed to take forever.

We finally arrived and went directly to our trip ending point where an outfitter was located. It was three miles north of Armstrong where we would end our trip. It had a nice landing and looked like a perfect ending place. We went back to the train station, bought our tickets, popped some tops, and waited for the train to arrive at 10:00 that night. We were all more than a little nervous about being dropped off, in the middle of the night, in the little town of Allenwater, to begin our journey at first light.

The topic of conversation centered on what the town of Allenwater was going to be like, while downing our excellent Canadian brews. The train finally arrived. We put our canoes, the rest of the beer, and all our gear in a boxcar, and loaded ourselves into a passenger car, and off we went. We caught a few winks on the train and before you know it, we were dropped off, in the middle of the night, in the middle of nowhere. I thought, *"Where's the town."* There is no town, just a platform to unload and a shed. *"Oh Boy,"* I thought. There is a lot of nothing with lots of mosquitoes. I looked over at Ellen who had a very worried look on her face. I said, *"Isn't this great, just look at all those stars."* Ellen said, *"Yeah right."* We tried unsuccessfully to sleep but did successfully drink the rest of the beer, which helped us greatly to endure the mosquitos that harassed us the rest of the night and eased any fears we had. And here is a little side note of wisdom we learned that night- It is possible to drink beer right through your mosquito head net. Let the excellent adventure begin.

ALLENWATER RIVER

We were all happy as clams to see the sun come up after an uncomfortable but fun night. I thought, *"If only Tuck had got us buzzed, the night we had to sleep under the stars, it would not have been so bad."* It was a beautiful brisk and bright Canadian morning and all our spirits instantly improved, well, maybe not all of us. Ellen still seemed a little nervous as she looked out at the Canadian Wilderness where we would spend the next 14 days traveling 130-miles and probably thought, *"What the hell did I get myself into?"* We loaded our canoes and Bill made a valid comment, that I was being excessively careful about my new boat. He said, *"It's going to be a long trip if you continue to be so paranoid about getting some scratches on your boat."* He had a point! It did not take us long to hit the first rapid and after two portages and several more rapids we found a great campsite and made an early camp. It was our lucky day; I caught a 5lb Walleye for dinner, and we proceeded to have our first awesome fish feed. And even Ellen had a smile on her face. We are off to a great start!

It was now Sunday, I got everyone up early, which I learned on the Missinaibi River, was so important for a successful trip, and noticed how relaxed Ellen and the rest of the team had become. We worked together well and managed to get on the river early. After experiencing the opposite with the Tuck river fiasco. And was a very good sign. We soon hit the next rapid, which had much bigger waves and was a little scary. Both boats took water but we made it through. We decided, with no arguments, to portage the next rapid, which had even bigger waves, and was really a small fall.

Typically, on a portage it takes two trips. First, we carry the packs over to get the lay of the land. Then, using two people, the front person with the tip of the canoe on their shoulder and the back person under the canoe resting it on their shoulders, carry it over the portage. This is a much easier and safer way to carry a big heavy tripping canoe. Remember how, Tuck Well, chose the macho method of one person carrying a heavy canoe. I believe this is a big mistake. It can lead to injury and great unhappiness, because of the effort it takes to carry a boat alone, both of which can ruin a trip. I have used this saying for years, *"It's not how fast you do a portage that matters. It's what you can do after a portage that counts."*

On the first trip over the trail, I saw a large bee hive that was just off the trail and warned everyone. We had no trouble until the last trip when Bill and I were carrying our boat over, when, to my great surprise, a large bee attacked me with uncanny viciousness, and promptly took a large hunk out of my arm. My arm swelled up like a grapefruit and it hurt like hell. I thought, *"Another lessoned learned, be more wary of large Canadian bees, they are bad asses and have only so much tolerance for trespassers."* I took some antihistamines from our medical kit to ease the allergic reaction and soaked my arm in the cold water for a while, and off we went.

The river widened out and we enjoyed some easy miles of marvelously calm water. We laughed at our good luck, always a bad idea, then the wind picked up and we got our first taste of paddling into the wind. Bummer, it was not so funny now. We did our fifth portage and found a nice camp after a short paddle through a little lake. Overall, it was not a bad second day, even with a painful bee sting, which was slowly getting better.

We had our first freeze-dried concoction for the trip, which turned out great, had a lively discussion around the fire and hit the rack early. Continuing with the routine of getting up early, on this fine Monday morning, we had a great start to the day with spirits high. We had a laugh when Billy gave the finger to a bush pilot flying over. We were now in Brennan Lake, which had a couple of fly-in fishing camps, and offered me my first orienteering challenge of the trip. We had to find the narrows and outlet to this part of the lake, and we were having a wee bit of trouble. I learned a lesson that day, to trust my compass and never go by dead reckoning. Dead reckoning, trying to look at the contours of the shoreline and lay of the land to figure out where you are, which lead to much heated debate between us traveling mates. We finally managed to find the outlet after paddling around awhile, and there was an intense rapid. The paddling partners were getting into a good rhythm, so we decided to paddle the first part and portage around the falls at the end. It proved to be very exciting and all of us did well, building confidence in our paddling skills. We camped there at a great site, and I noticed how the group was jelling together. Everyone knew what had to be done and pitched right in and got the job done fast. It is great when this happens on a canoe trip. All people need is a little direction on what to do and then naturally everything falls into place making for a very enjoyable trip. The next morning, we decided to fish below the falls and proceeded to catch some nice walleyes. We were ahead of schedule, and decided to spend the rest of the morning cooking and feasting on fish. Life is just great sometimes, enjoying the spoils of the wilderness.

We left that afternoon with spirits high and headed for Granite Falls. After three hours and an easy rapid, we found the falls. Granite Falls was big. We could hear its roar from a long way off, and proceeded with great caution as we approached it. I remembered the man who went over Thunder House Falls on the Missinaibi River. Going over a fall of this size is a sure way for an early grave.

WILDERNESS EMERGENCY OR STUPIDITY?

We knew the portage trail, from our maps, was on the right side of the falls so we hugged that bank. To our surprise at the portage trail, we found a fishing boat along with a distress note, describing the predicament five paddlers found themselves in. The note described how one of their two canoes had swamped down stream, in Little Sturgeon Rapids, causing them to lose their boat and one food pack. They related that one member of their party had sustained a knee injury during the incident. They stated that they were working their way up river and planned to use this fishing boat, they had borrowed from a fly-in camp, to get everyone back to the camp and had arranged to be flown out. They asked for any help that we could provide. We grabbed our packs to start our portage when low and behold; here comes a man carrying a large pack walking up the portage trail. I had a good comprehensive medical kit, so the first thing I asked the man was; *"Who's hurt? Maybe we could help with that!"* He said, *"I'm the one I banged my knee."* *"What,"* I thought, *"You couldn't be hurt too badly, if you can carry a large heavy pack up a bad portage trail, and I relaxed."* He then began to relate their story to us.

"We are a group of five paddlers in two canoes on a fifty-mile trip. We are from Illinois and I am a professor at the University of Illinois and planned the trip. We decided to run Little Sturgeon Rapids where my canoe, with three people and a large food pack had swamped in large waves. The canoe pack sank, I banged my knee and the canoe went flying down the river." He seemed to be reveling in relating this wilderness emergency. He continued, *"We shuttled and portaged people and gear over two trips, paddled back up river to this portage trail and camped. We took the remaining boat and paddled to a fly-in fishing camp where we borrowed a boat and arranged to be flown out."* I then asked him, *"What kind of canoe did you loose?"* He said, *"A brand new 17-foot Grumman canoe."* I said, *"Did you try and find it down river?"* He replied, *"No, I knew it was lost, and we have had enough! If you find it, you can have it."* I thought *"OH BOY!"*

My experience had taught me that a canoe that has tipped in a rapid, and as long as it was not pinned, could probably be recovered. I also thought, this person was a real Dick Wad, just like another person I knew. HA! He was more interested in a great wilderness emergency story than making this a great canoe trip. *"Oh well,"* and thought to each his own. And too bad for the people who had trusted him on this trip. But then again, a great story makes for an unforgettable trip.

To all of you who may have an interest in paddling in the wilderness, there is a lot to learn from our wilderness friends. First, this is a good example of how going light is important in canoe tripping. The heavier a canoe is the more unstable it is and the easier it will tip over. As I said before, three people in a canoe is a bad idea. Second, every pack should float. We pack waterproof bags in each of our big Duluth type packs and make sure that each pack has a ground pad in it, which will float the pack by itself, like a cork. Our packs make awesome rafts, which I have utilized more than once when flying down the river after a capsize. Third, each canoe should have flotation bags in each end making them float like a cork, which will help prevent them from pinning or trapping someone behind them. As you have learned, a big tripping canoe can hold as much as 200 gallons of water, and at 8 lbs a gallon that is 1600 whopping pounds flying down the

river. With the force of the water and its weight, a canoe can easily be destroyed or unrecoverably pinned. "*Yikes!*" In later years on other expeditions, we would use canoe covers transforming a tripping canoe into a big kayak. The end float bags, along with the packs, which float well, performs like a boat completely filled with flotation and is much safer. Being up the river without a paddle is bad, being in the wilderness without a boat is an emergency. Fourth, if you do not have the knowledge and the gear and cannot sustain a tip over on a wilderness trip without losing your boat, gear or food, you might want to think hard about doing the trip. I am on my high horse now, but you know I learned from doing everything wrong, and wonder sometimes how I am still around. So, do it if you must or heed this old guide's advice.

We walked the Granite Falls canoe portage and discovered we could shorten the portage by putting in at the edge of the falls, cutting the portage in half. There was a giant eddy there, making the put in easy, but cutting through the strong eddy line, we discovered, was not an easy task at all. Bill and I loaded our canoe and paddled out only to be bounced back by the strong eddy line. And after several frustrating attempts, we tried aggressively cutting through the current. This got us through, but were instantly spun around by the current and almost tipped over. We discovered that day that you have to cut through the eddy line current aggressively and the front person has to do a draw or cross draw leaning aggressively down stream to prevent a tip over. This is called a peel out. The draw or cross draw stroke catches the current, which you can lean on, raising the up-stream gunnel, and preventing a tip over.

As we were battling our way out of the eddy, we all noticed the fins that were breaking the surface in the foam from the falls. *"Wow, those fins are walleye fins. Let's try and find a place close to camp,"* I exclaimed. We found a great spot to camp across the bay from the falls and spent the next day catching fish and catching our breaths. It is important on a wilderness trip not to get behind schedule, and if you are ahead of schedule, which you should always be, you should take the time to enjoy what the wilderness has to offer. I try hard to get ahead of schedule and always plan a layover day each week. The fishing is almost always good below a fall and cooking up fresh fish is a real treat. In the morning that day I caught a large northern, about 10lbs, after losing six. I caught this fish in a unique way. I had hooked a nice walleye, had it almost to shore, when a big 10lb northern chomped down on it, and refused to let go. Bad decision by the Pike; greed will get you every time. A good way to cook a big fish like that Pike is to clean it but do not filet it. Salt the inside of the fish well, then find a suitable stick to put through its mouth and butt, and suspend it over a low fire to cook slowly. The fish is done when its flesh easily falls off the bones. What fun it is, to let our savage side out, picking at the fish right off the stick with one's fingers.

Chris and Ellen had decided to go paddle early that evening and find a place to catch some more fish. When they returned, I noticed some tension between Chris and Ellen, who appeared to be shook up. I took Chris aside and asked him what was up. He said, *"Ellen and I decided to try some fishing a little down stream, when suddenly she freaked out. She started to scream that we have to turn back right now. She was totally hysterical man. I couldn't believe it."* "Wow," I said. He continued, *"Finally I calmed her down and we paddled back."* I asked, *"Is she alright now?"* Chris replied, *"Yeah, she just got scared that we would not be able to get back."*

It is very important to remember that fear can be lurking just under the surface on a wilderness trip. This is especially true if you have not traveled much in the wilderness, as Ellen had not. Fear is a very powerful emotion that can overcome any logic. The guide or trip leader must be aware of this and do everything possible to keep those powerful emotions at bay. You should all remember what fear did on the Tuck Well trip. When the entire group, except Bill and I, turned back and went up stream through some horrible conditions and then walked out. All while Bill and I had the time of our life finishing the trip.

CANOE?

With much anticipation, of what the day would bring, we woke up to a cold and gray day. *"Not to worry,"* I exclaimed *"most of the time this turns into a beautiful sunny day."* We had two big questions on our minds. Is little Sturgeon Rapids going to eat us up, like our new Wilderness Emergency friends? And, more importantly will we find their canoe as I had anticipated? Surprise, we had a portage right off the bat. Nobody said anything about that. It was short and no trouble and we soon came to Little Sturgeon Rapids. We eddied out, a great way to check out rapids, and took a peek. It didn't look bad at all, so Bill and I made the run first with no troubles. It had some big waves that our not-overloaded boat handled well. Chris and Ellen then came through; they took on a little water, but made it fine. We went around the corner and across a little bay; we all spotted a beautiful shiny object, which I knew was that new Grumman canoe. I thought," *Was it damaged beyond repair?*" We all headed for it with excited anticipation. It had floated right up to a beach. We landed and checked the boat out. There was not a scratch on the canoe, it was in perfect shape. We all thought, *"Why didn't they retrieve the boat, it was only a short distance from where they dumped, literally right around the corner and across a little bay."* Well, our gain and I guess a great story was worth it to the Professor. At least he created a great adventure story for himself, but not so great memories for the people who were with him. However, like I said, those adventurous times are the ones that are unforgettable, but their memories would have been a lot better if they had finished the trip.

We answered two of our questions, now we had to figure out what to do with a third canoe. This was the exact boat we had paddled in on the Missinaibi River and the friend's boat I helped wreck, maybe not wreck but put a good hurt on it. Remember, we were able to get it mostly back in shape, on the Wolf River in Wisconsin. A Standard 17-foot Grumman is not a bad boat and has recently been put back into production. It does not stand up as well as the modern boats like the Old Town Tripper that I had just purchased, but this was free for the taking with the blessing of the owner. SO!!! We had 90 miles still to go, four people and three canoes. Can we tow it? We tried that. Not so good! *"How about soloing two of the boats?"* I suggested, *"We could take turns?"* None of us had really soloed much, but we were young and full of XXXX and decided to give it a try.

When you solo a canoe the ideal position of the seat is about 15" behind center. This allows you to reach the front and back of the canoe which helps you steer. It also slightly raises the nose of the canoe, which also helps you steer. Let me explain this a little more. The reason why it takes two people to steer a canoe and why as you solo you need to reach the front and back is simple physics. When you have current or wind there is a force on your canoe. If the force is directly behind you, it simply pushes you forward. Nothing wrong with that, but if the force hits you from the side, say you get a little turned, then that force is transferred to the whole side of the canoe. If you can picture in your mind wind hitting the side of your canoe; one person, say the back, would be fighting this force to try to straighten the canoe out, but it would help the front person by pushing the canoe the way you want to go. To make this clearer, take a pencil and use your finger to push the back then push the front. You can see how it will be easy for one and hard for the other to steer a canoe. Your finger represents the force; one helps turn

the boat and one resists. If none of this makes any sense, simply remember that 50% of the time either the front or the back person will have great trouble steering the canoe. Both front and back paddlers have to be able to steer the canoe. This is a basic principle of paddling, unfortunately, we did not have this basic principle down at this stage in our development and we did not have a center seat in the canoe. Therefore, things were not as easy as we anticipated.

We did know enough to turn the boat around and paddle from the front seat backwards getting us closer to the middle but that was the extent of our expertise at 27 years old. I took the Grumman and Bill took the Montgomery Ward canoe and, Chris and Ellen took the Tripper. We soon came to Big Sturgeon Falls and portaged, and realized it would now take longer with the three boats. I then thought, *"This canoe ain't going to be free. We are going to have to work like hell to get it back."* The paddling was easy down this stretch of river with no problems. We found a nice campsite close to the big lake we would hit the next morning.

We had been eating a lot of freeze-dried food and decided to change things up with some jerky soup for dinner. I started the soup with homemade beef jerky, which is great for lunches, by soaking it in water over a slow fire. After it reconstituted back into tasty spicy beef, I added Manischewitz, a dry vegetable soup mix, and some dried potatoes. I then made some corn bread, out of a just-add-water mix, in our tote oven and viola, a grand meal, which was enjoyed by all.

Planning food for a canoe trip is one of the biggest challenges. It has to be light, nutritious, filling, easy to cook and tasty. Freeze dried food has improved greatly over the years, but should never be considered to be a complete meal out of the bag. It is only the basic part of making a great meal. I always add extra ingredients and spices. You can add extra noodles, rice, potatoes, dried meats, fish, powdered cheese, dried fruit, spices, or whatever your culinary imagination can create. I start by looking at the ingredients in the freeze-dried meal and compliment these. I always try to keep it as simple as possible. A good example would be adding extra dried vegetables to a freeze-dried beef stew and serving it over instant mashed potatoes.

When I cook, I always start by soaking the freeze-dried meal in warm water. The longer the food soaks, the better it will reconstitute. This is especially true for any meats or poultry.

I find a lot of food to make into tasty meals right in my local supper market. All noodles are dried, as are rice, potatoes, and even some meats, and I always think light. Breakfast and lunch should be simple. We eat a lot of oatmeal for breakfast, and use cereal and pancakes for a change of pace, adding dried fruit to all. Getting a dehydrator and making your own dried fruit and vegetables is a great way to go. A bushel of apples makes a couple of real light bags of fruit that go a long way on a trip. For lunch, we eat jerky, trail mix, dried corn, granola bars, cheese crackers, fruit, cookies and more. We eat three meals a day with snacks in between, but always follow a planned amount every day even on the last day. Remember! You never know when you will get off the river until you are off the river. Don't eat all your food the last night!

Losing your food on a canoe trip would be a real bummer. Our new wilderness friends had lost part of their food, because one of their packs deep sixed, and probably was one of the reasons they bugged out. We always double bag our food and then put it into a good waterproof bag or pack. This obviously keeps it dry, but it also contains the smell of the food. This is important because animals have great noses. If a mouse smells food in your pack, it will chew right through your pack to get at it. We always try to hang our food packs off the ground to keep them safe. A good way to accomplish that is to use a throw rope (rescue bag), a small bag of rope used for river rescue which I always bring. And can easily be thrown over a tree branch. It is designed to be thrown and works great for this purpose. If there are no trees, we put the food pack on top of a canoe, which makes a great table using rocks or logs under gunwales on the ends, and booby trap it with our cook kit. I set my tent up strategically close, to be alerted if something is after it. You might be wondering what I would do if it was a bear. Well, I would get out of the tent screaming, generally acting like a wild man waving my hands and jumping up and down. You may be thinking now, yeah right. Ok, here is a true story. When we were developing our resort in the early nineties, we had parked the GMC, in a clearing on the property as our home. Well, one morning there was a black bear getting into our garbage. It knocked it over and made a giant mess. The next morning the same 400lb bear revisited us again at 5:30 in the morning, and this time I had had enough. I jumped outside in my underwear, grabbed a big rock while screaming and began to chase the bear, which must have been impressed by this wild creature chasing it. It then stopped, looked back and I kept coming, then the bear took off like it had been bit in the ass by a badger. Now, if this had been a grizzly bear, my actions would have been much different. I would have quietly let the bear have the garbage. The saying goes; you can kick a black bear in the ass, but a grizzly will kick your ass. Don't get me wrong, bears can be potentially dangerous, so use your own common sense when you decide what action to take and never hassle a momma bear with a cub.

It was now Friday, day 7 of our trip. We had a pleasant morning paddling the dead calm of Wabakimi Lake. I thought, *"This will be a cake walk."* NOT! When we came to Lower Wabakimi Lake, the wind picked up. If you have ever have paddled a canoe with the front sticking up in the air in a stiff wind you may have an understanding of what it was like. Well, I made some cool circles as the wind spun me around like a top, and I barely made it to a small patch of land and stopped. I asked, *"How do you like my great panoramic boat?"* They were all getting a good laugh out of my performance. Now what? I noticed that Bill did not have the same trouble that I had. HMM! We have a long way to go and I could barely make it 200 yards in this wind. I thought *"There's no way I'm going to leave this damn canoe, it must be the weight in Bill's boat that helped push his front end down and helped him to not get blown around in circles. Duh!* I begged for some of their gear, and put it in the front and I tried it again. Off we went with much better results but the progress was slow, very slow, but we made it to a small piece of land and hoped the wind would die down. We waited awhile and then moved about 200 yards to a small campsite and continued to wait for the wind to die. It never did and we stayed all night. *"Thank God I'm bushed," I thought."*

Most days, unless a storm was coming in, the wind picked up somewhere around 10:00 in the morning. After the agony with the wind, we endured the day before, we got up before daybreak and hoped to make some easy miles before the wind picked up again. Chris and I took the solo boats for this stretch and we managed to make about a third of the way across the lake when here comes the damn wind again, a lot earlier than planned. What, it's not in our faces, it's at our backs. What a great day it was becoming, cheers went up all around, even with the coming cold wind at our backs. We literally flew down the lake and even used our paddles as make-shift sails. Things were looking up. We ran some easy rapids and then came to a fall we had to portage. We were making great time, so we took the time to fish the next falls leading into Smooth Rock Lake. Remember, it is good fishing below falls. It did not take long before both Billy and I caught the biggest walleyes of the trip. We got into Smooth Rock Lake again with wind at our backs and camped before the last open stretch of lake. With another great walleye dinner in our bellies, we managed to get to bed just before the storm hit. What a great day!

It was now Sunday and we got up to some damn wind, thanks to said storm during the night and *"UH OH!"* We all thought, especially the ones soloing, it had changed directions and we were looking at one hard pull today. That turned out to be a gross understatement. After we acquired the third canoe, it put a new dynamic on the trip. We were not totally convinced that we would be able to paddle the third canoe out, but we were hell bent to try. Bill and Chris were the solo canoeists that day and spent the day fighting big waves and tortuous winds that forced us south off our course. Luckily, we didn't make a mistake and take the wrong channel out of the lake. Thank the gods for a compass! Everyone was tired and cold and then the Canadian low decided to move along and we enjoyed a beautiful campsite and peaceful evening with beautiful magenta skies.

Getting up early and traveling hard again, had put us ahead of schedule, even with the terrible conditions that we endured at times. We knew we were on course to finish the trip in the time that we had allotted, no matter what the weather would throw at us. It is not pretty when a group turns to the negative as it did on the Missinaibi trip with Tuck Well as the guide. I guess I should thank him for that, otherwise I may not have learned such an important lesson. Again, what a joy it was to be part of group that was so positive. We all had such a positive attitude; we felt we could conquer the world.

We had plenty of time, and with the knowledge of how important early starts were, by choice, the next morning, everyone decided to skip breakfast and get a jump on the wind. The wind of course, Murphy's Law, Murphy must have been a hell of an unlucky guy, never picked up. We made great time through the rest of Smooth Rock, Caribou and Funger Lakes and were looking forward to paddling down the Caribou River, our next destination. Ellen commented, *"With the wind at our backs I feel like Queen Sheba being carried on her gondola out for on an idol stroll."* We were looking for an outlet out of the lake when, *"What's this?"* Chris shouted, *"We're at the outlet which was an inlet, something is not right here."* I checked my map and, *"OH Boy! We have to go up the Caribou River"*, I exclaimed. Thoughts of Queen Sheba quickly faded, and of course, bad luck Murphy stepped in and the rain started coming down in buckets. Things were looking bleak at this point and then we spotted a nice campsite just before the river, and headed for it. I bet we were not the first people to spend a night here contemplating their fate. We had a nice tarp with us for just these occasions. Another great use of one of the two throw ropes we had with us, was to use it as a ridgeline for the tarp. With its sixty-foot length it is easy to find two trees to string it across and then stake down to make a great shelter. Once the shelter was up, and a nice meal in our bellies, the mood quickly improved and we were all looking forward to the challenge the next day would bring.

It was now Tuesday and off we went to conquer the Caribou River. None of us had ever paddled up stream before, but Bill and I remembered how our group had on the rock gardens of the Missinaibi River. If they could do that, we certainly could do this and we did. We went right up the rapid pulling our boats with 25-foot lining lines we had on each end, and it was easy. This is a great way to travel up a rapid. It takes a little practice and you have to secure the lines well when not in use preventing any entangled in the event of a tip over. The other most important thing to remember about lining is to let go of your end if the boat gets sideways!

ORIENTEERING

We were now heading for Outlet Bay via the large Caribou Lake and saw on the map what we thought would be a good short cut, where a little river went into Little Caribou Lake. The big question of the day was; is there a portage trail there? We all realized that we were now traveling down hill again and getting into Little Caribou Lake via this little river would be a lot better than the possibility of fighting a 50 mile an hour wind down the large part of Caribou Lake, which was our other choice. The added bonus is we would end up closer to Armstrong where we parked the truck at the outfitters landing. We decided to take a chance, and give it a try.

I had been progressively getting better at orienteering but I knew this would be a challenge with the many islands, channels, and bends to navigate. I had made a few mistakes along the way. None was too serious and all of them had to do with dead reckoning and not trusting the compass. The good news, for this area, is the declination is almost zero so I would not have to worry about that. Declination is the difference between true north and magnetic north, which could amount to a lot. If the declination is 10 degrees east, you have to subtract from your heading. If the declination is 10 degrees west, you have to add to your heading. Here is a little saying that helps me remember this; if the declination is east compass least and if the declination is west compass best.

I knew exactly where we were and made the decision, not to trust anything that I saw but, simply trust my compass and only go by the bearings that I took. That also meant I had to ignore all the input from the other dead reckoning experts that I was with, which turned out to be the harder of the two.

To make a bearing, you lay your compass on the map and line up the north lines with the north lines on the compass, then you turn the compass to the point where you want to go. This will give you a bearing. Picking up the compass, putting the north needle in the north place on the compass, you sight something in the distance and paddle to that point. When you get there, you repeat the process until you hopefully arrive at your destination. I did just that and then exclaimed, "*I can't believe it*!" I thought, with joy there it was, a portage trail up a steep hill. This was a cathartic moment for me, which has served me well in the next thirty-five years of wilderness tripping. Cheers went up by my mates all around and we portaged into a little river and soon made it, after a long rewarding day, to a nice campsite where my fellow voyageurs affectionately named this pass "Rohr's Pass."

It was now Wednesday, the eleventh day of our trip, and with mixed feelings, we all knew we were near trails end. After an easy paddle down Little Caribou Lake, we arrived at the landing. We now had to figure out how to get the couple of miles back to the truck. Luck was with us that day as a local woman in a pickup truck offered to give us a ride back to Armstrong. Bill, Ellen and I jumped in, Chris stayed back with the gear to snooze and dream of burgers and beer, and off we went. The trip was great except for the nefarious smells in the back of truck. And we were soon dumped back in Armstrong at the GMC. We drove back to get

Chris and the gear. It did not take us long to pack our gear but we had not yet figured out how we would get the hard-fought boat home. Bill exclaimed, *"Are we going to have to leave this boat, which took so much effort to get? How the heck are we going to get three boats on top of the GMC rack which was designed for two?"* I said, *"No way are we going to leave this boat."* My friend Leonard, the black smith, built this rack very strong. It could carry ten boats. I said, *"Let's match up the two canoes that are most alike and we will tie the third one on top between the two."* We put the Grumman and Tripper on the bottom with the Montgomery Ward canoe on the top between both, tied her down, and we were on the road by 5:00 pm on a quest for some burgers and ice, we already had beer but it was warm after two weeks in the GMC!

HOME

Now after 23 hours, 160 miles of a dirty and dusty gravel road, 600 miles of every other kind of road, burgers, more beer, breezing across the border, getting lost in the fog and sleeping like a dog, we arrived back home.

We were left a little bit battered and a little bit burnt, savoring the mingling memories, both good and bad of every moment of this great wilderness adventure. The clock fell off the dashboard but it is still ticking August 24th 1977 2:43pm. If you want great memories, you have to have excellent adventures.

REFLECTIONS

The idea for Rohr's Wilderness Tours was hatched in the back of the GMC on the way home from the Allenwater trip. It was not until 1983, after several more wilderness adventures of large proportion, that it became a reality.

As we get older, reflection becomes an important past time. I thought it would be fun to bring you these reflections in a book. And just maybe, you got a chuckle and a bit of wisdom from the dumb ass mistakes that helped me become the seasoned guide that I am today. Last but not the least, if you want to have great memories you have to have excellent adventures. Now get off your duffs and make some of your own!

Printed in the USA
CPSIA information can be obtained
at www.ICGtesting.com
LVHW080753110424
776968LV00014B/711